MONUMENT VALLEY

NAVAJO TRIBAL PARK
AND
THE NAVAJO RESERVATION

NICKY LEACH

SIERRA PRESS
MARIPOSA, CA

DEDICATION

For the Navajo, who have a lot to teach the rest of us about living well in this world. Their quiet, reverential, and enduring spirit is best captured in this prayer:

> Beauty before me,
> > With it I wander.
> Beauty behind me,
> > With it I wander.
> Beauty before me,
> > With it I wander.
> Beauty below me,
> > With it I wander.
> Beauty above me,
> > With it I wander.
> Beauty all around me,
> > With it I wander.
> In old age traveling,
> > With it I wander.
> On the beautiful trail I am,
> > With it I wander.

From *First Song of Dawn Boy*

INSIDE FRONT COVER
The Mittens silhouetted by a dramatic sunrise, Monument Valley. PHOTO ©DICK DIETRICH
PAGE 2
Buttes of Monument Valley seen through Tear Drop Arch. PHOTO ©LARRY CARVER
TITLE PAGE
Young Navajo girl holding a baby goat, near Ganado, Arizona. PHOTO ©FRED HIRSCHMANN
OPPOSITE
Totem Pole and the Yei Bi Chei rocks, Monument Valley. PHOTO ©CHUCK LAWSEN
BELOW
Nineteenth-century Navajo pictographs in Canyon del Muerto, Canyon de Chelly National Monument. PHOTO ©FRED HIRSCHMANN

CONTENTS

OPPOSITE
Three Sisters and distant forms of Hunt's Mesa,
Monument Valley. PHOTO ©TOM TILL
BELOW
Sacred datura in bloom. PHOTO ©GEORGE H. H. HUEY

7

WELCOME TO NAVAJOLAND

Hogan in Monument Valley, early morning.   PHOTO ©TOM TILL

It's sunset on a cool October evening when the Chevy Suburban pulls up outside a sprawling homestead near Torreon in the southeastern corner of the Navajo Nation. My two Navajo guides—seniors working as part of Cuba High School Travel Academy's unique cultural tourism program—introduce me to Pasqualita Toledo, a recent graduate, and her family. After touring Chaco Canyon all afternoon, I will be staying in one of their hogans tonight, sharing the space with their brother's girlfriend. She and the youngest Toledo boys are watching a movie inside the hogan, seated on an old couch, giggling shyly as I enter.

The hogan is typical of thousands on the reservation. It's circular with a hard dirt floor, a roof hole, a wood stove for heat, and a door on the east, facing the sunrise. I unroll my sleeping bag on a bed on the west side, traditionally reserved for guests, place a water bottle by the door, and go for a walk. The Toledo outfit, set at the edge of a pretty mesa, has a frame house and two hogans, and a spectacular view of Cabezon Peak in the Rio Puerco valley. I take all this in from a doorless outhouse standing on its own between the hogan and the cliffs. My every move is watched by curious goats and sheep in a nearby corral. Several ducks floating on a pond start squawking as I return to the hogan. The cacophony bounces off sandstone walls, the only sound for miles around.

Over a supper of Navajo tacos, an Indian staple consisting of piping hot frybread topped with meat, cheese, and salsa, I talk to Pasqualita and her sisters and brother. They are a large family, 12 in all. Most are unmarried and still living at home, helping their parents, Peter and Evelyn, with chores. After losing his hearing, Peter recently retired from the railroad and money is tight. The older girls and a brother work at the new Hyatt Regency Tamaya Resort in Bernalillo owned by Santa Ana Pueblo. They leave at 5 a.m. each morning in their brother's car and commute an hour, work for 12 hours, and return to the hogan at 7 p.m.

Although they are tired, they are intrigued by this stranger in their midst. The young boys stare at me, like all children fascinated by anyone who looks and sounds different. The girls tell me stories about their *kinaaldas*, the Navajo puberty ceremony honoring Changing Woman, when each girl comes of age. "It's tiring but fun," says one. "Grinding corn and making the cake was the best bit," confides another. They look at me without comprehension when I tell them I live in Santa Fe. Although it is just on the other side of the Jemez Mountains, none of them has ever been there.

In fact, although US 550, the main road between Albuquerque and Bloomfield, is just a few miles to the west, the vast Navajo Nation is a world unto itself. More than 300,000 people live here, amid the sagebrush mesas and river canyons between the four sacred mountains. Even those Navajos who live in modern housing in towns bordering the reservation return regularly to family land, where relatives still raise corn and livestock. Navajo women, the powerhouses of this matriarchal society, count their wealth in sheep and goats, which provide food and wool for weaving into rugs.

Even so, there is a growing linguistic and cultural divide among the traditional, deeply religious "longhairs" and youngsters between the ages of 19 and 38 who now make up more than half the population. Many younger people speak no Navajo, a language so complex and hard to understand it was used in World War II for coded messages that helped America and its allies win the war. But without the language, the Navajo culture, enshrined in stories and chants taught on long winter nights, cannot be passed on to the next generation, whose attention is more easily captured nowadays by television, the Internet, and American culture. It's a dilemma of which the Navajo tribe is all too aware.

The Navajo have lived in the Southwest for at least 500 years, with recent archaeological evidence pushing back the date to A.D. 1000. The Dineh, or The People, as they call themselves, were nomads of the Athapascan culture who came from northwestern Canada so long ago they now tell of always being here. While their Apache relatives remained hunter-gatherers, the Navajo became pastoralists, learning farming, weaving, and pottery from the Pueblos, who named them *navaju*, "people of the great cultivated fields."

Spectacular Spider Rock, late afternoon, Canyon de Chelly National Monument.

Throughout the Spanish and Mexican periods (1598–1821), Navajos fiercely resisted the colonization that had defeated most of the Pueblos but eagerly adapted European innovations for their own purposes. They raided settlements for horses, goats, and sheep, learned silversmithing, and began building outdoor ovens. When the Southwest became U.S. territory in 1846, even the relentless government campaign that ended in the Navajos' horrendous 1864 incarceration at Fort Sumner did not defeat them. After signing the 1868 treaty that created the Navajo reservation, several thousand Dineh returned home with a few livestock and a handful of trade goods and began to rebuild. With mixed feelings, they adopted Anglo education, material goods, political organization, and resource development, all of which have made the tribe one of the wealthiest and best-educated in the country. But they remain fiercely independent. No amount of setbacks, it appears, can deter such a people, for whom nothing is more important than clan, religion, and the land they call their own.

Early the next morning, I leave the Toledo homestead, after breakfasting on scrambled eggs, homestyle potatoes, and fruit rustled up by Peter Toledo. As I leave, everyone gathers around a freshly butchered sheep, which Peter and his son slaughtered as we sat inside eating. It will keep the Toledos in mutton stew for a week or more, and every piece of the animal will be used. Despite the TV, the kung fu posters, the kid's Spiderman pajamas, and tubs of Blue Bonnet margarine in the fridge, this is an America that few Anglos experience. For those of us that have, it offers a window into another world and a reflection on our own that remains in the memory forever. Every encounter on the Navajo reservation offers an opportunity for such experiences, if you're willing to take the time to get to know the people for whom this is truly home.

ILLUSTRATION BY DARLECE CLEVELAND

Most of the Navajo reservation is in northeastern Arizona, extending into New Mexico and Utah—an area known popularly as the Four Corners. It is bounded on the south by Interstate 40, on the north by US 160 and 64, on the east by US 550, and on the west by US 89. Roads cross the main waterways of the Navajo reservation: the Colorado, Little Colorado, and Paria; the San Juan and Animas; and the Rio Grande and Puerco Rivers. Once filled with dusty, rutted roads, the Navajo Nation is today easily accessible to travelers.

The towering, volcanic peaks, distinctive, winding sandstone mesas, and river-cut canyons that characterize the Navajo reservation are a feature of the Colorado Plateau, the 130,000-square-mile uplift in which the reservation sits. The Colorado Plateau averages 5,200 feet high and is mostly contained within Utah, with small portions in Colorado, New Mexico, and Arizona.

On the south, the Colorado Plateau begins at the 2,000-foot-high Mogollon Rim, the basaltic highland that transects north-central Arizona and southwest New Mexico. Its eastern boundary is the region west of Colorado's Rocky Mountains and their southern extension—the Sandia and Sangre de Cristo Mountains—along New Mexico's Rio Grande rift valley. On the north, the boundary is Utah's Uinta Mountains. The western boundary is entirely in Utah and follows the Wasatch Mountains near Salt Lake City south, past the High Plateaus of central Utah, to the Grand Wash Cliffs.

Localized uplifts split the region into distinctive highlands known as the Coconino, Kaibab, Kanab, Shivwits, Kaibito, Defiance, and Paria Plateaus—a colorful, up-and-down, topsy-turvy landscape known as Canyon Country. Here, within a 250-mile radius you'll find 12 national parks, 14 national monuments, 7 tribal parks, 17 wilderness areas, seven state parks, and six national forests, making up what visitors' bureaus dub "The Grand Circle".

Geology is the focus at the Grand Canyon, Zion, Canyonlands, Arches, Capitol Reef, and Bryce Canyon National Parks, Natural Bridges, Cedar Breaks, and Grand Staircase-Escalante National Monuments, and Glen Canyon National Recreation Area. Chaco Culture National Historical Park, Mesa Verde National Park, and Hovenweep, Aztec Ruins, Bandelier, and Pipe Spring National Monuments tell human stories. Within and bordering the Navajo Nation, Canyon de Chelly, Rainbow Bridge, Petrified Forest, El Malpais, El Morro, Wupatki, Sunset Crater, and Navajo National Monuments and Hubbell Trading Post National Historic Site preserve both scenery and culture. Tribal parks operated by the Navajos, Utes, and Paiutes add their own distinctive voice to the mix—preserving archaeological remains, extraordinary scenery, lakes, forests, wildlife, and historic sites, all of it interpreted entirely from the Indian point of view.

PAGE 12/13: The floor of Monument Valley as seen from North Window. PHOTO ©BRUCE HUCKO

To a Navajo, every rock formation in *Dine Bikeyah*, Navajo Country, has a story. Here is the verdant side canyon that nurtured The People while they were hiding from Kit Carson during the Long Walk. Down there is the rock spire where Spider Woman taught the first Navajo to weave. And over there, on the far horizon, are the volcanic crags that are the petrified remains of monsters slain by the Hero Twins during the creation of this, the Fifth World.

Western scientific explanations for why this landscape looks the way it does seem prosaic in comparison. Beginning about 4.5 billion years ago, rocks were laid down as sediments in a succession of volcanic explosions, warm oceans, windblown sandy beaches, and meandering rivers, then contorted by earthquakes, uplifted into ridges, and worn down by erosion into the strange anthropomorphic-looking landmarks we see today.

According to our notions, sacred peaks such as Navajo Mountain in the northern reservation, are in fact laccoliths, humpbacked mountains pushed up by volcanic eruptions that never reached the surface. The petrified eagle monster whose body is now Ship Rock is a volcanic plug, uncovered by erosion. And Owl Rock, Three Sisters, The Mittens, and other Monument Valley landmarks were actually carved by differential erosion—the miraculous ability of wind, water, ice, and gravity to shape rock according to its hardness into shapes that have given us our "story rocks" of today.

BEGINNINGS

The Navajo reservation lies entirely within the southern one-third of the mile-high Colorado Plateau, a 130,000-square-mile geophysical province of relatively flat-lying sedimentary rocks dotted with broad folds and uplifts, two huge basins, and the remnants of countless volcanoes, some as young as

a million years old. Four states meet within its boundaries: northeastern Arizona, southeastern Utah, northwestern New Mexico, and southwestern Colorado.

The wrench-faults that squeezed up the Colorado Plateau are ancient, more than 1.5 billion years old, dating back to Precambrian time. But they did not begin pushing up Plateau Country until about 65 million years ago, when a major collision of the Pacific and North American tectonic plates, off the coast of California, sent shock waves eastward, elevating the Rocky Mountains and major uplifts such as the Monument Upwarp in which Monument Valley has been eroded.

Rocks are hardened, or lithified, by compression from younger sediments deposited on them, one atop the other, over eons. Throughout the Paleozoic Era (570–250 million years ago), the basement rocks of the Navajo Reservation were laid down in and around a large, long-lived, tropical inland seaway. Sand along the ocean shoreline hardened into sandstone, offshore muddy sediments became shale loaded with trilobites, and the calcareous bodies of sea creatures dying in the ocean became thick beds of limestone.

At the start of the Pennsylvanian Period (325

million years ago), the inland sea withdrew further west. About this time, the Ancestral Rockies and other mountain chains began to rise along faults, accompanied by huge neighboring mountain basins. In southeastern Utah, miles of salt and gypsum formed in the Paradox Basin as the sea dried up; these minerals were then buried by a succession of pale shoreline sands, red riverine sediments washed down from the Uncompaghre Uplift to the east, and later sediments. Under this overburden, the Paradox salts became mobile, moved away from the weight, then released their pressure along faults. North of the San Juan River, you can see the result: numerous fractured salt domes, where groundwater has washed out the salt, exposing the underlying sandstones to erosion by wind and water into the linear salt valleys, arches, fins, and spires of Canyon Country.

A MIDDLE-AGED LANDSCAPE

At the end of the Paleozoic Era, during the Permian Period, the sea once again expanded into the region west of Navajo Country, leaving behind Elephant Canyon Formation limestone and red Halgaito Shale (Navajo for "a spring in the open valley"), both visible along the San Juan River, near Mexican Hat. As the Mesozoic Era dawned, a long period of desertification affected the West, and shoreline sands blew into high, cross-bedded dunes, laying down the Cutler Group formations. In southeastern Utah, the creamy Cedar Mesa Sandstone covers the Elephant Canyon and Halgaito Formations, all of which have been uncovered by erosion within the last several million years by the San Juan River. The ledgy red siltstone known as Organ Rock forms the pedestal for the monuments in Monument Valley. Above it, the De Chelly Sandstone, named for its beautiful outcroppings in the cliffs of Canyon de Chelly, is

---

ABOVE: The dramatic laccolithic form of Agathla Peak (also known as *El Capitan*) south of Monument Valley, sunrise. PHOTO ©DICK DIETRICH

wind-sculpted into numerous forms in Monument Valley.

Above the Cutler Group are formations that are found mainly in the Western Reservation. Chocolate brown mudstones and siltstones of the Moenkopi Formation are best seen near Tuba City. Above the Moenkopi is the Chinle Formation, consisting of crumbly, variegated mudstones, siltstones, and some sandstone and limestone that becomes brilliantly colored after a heavy rain. It is the Chinle that gives the Painted Desert, south of Black Mesa, its beautiful rainbow hues.

Fossilized dinosaur bones and wood are a common occurrence in this formation. Petrified wood was created when tall pines fell and were entombed in riverine mud. Ash from volcanic eruptions in the Mogollon Rim region, south of what is now Petrified Forest National Park, mixed with groundwater as silica and seeped into the buried wood, replacing the cambium with bright jasper, quartz, and other crystals.

The return of an even longer period of deserts and hot, dry conditions is evident in major exposures of Triassic-era sandstones of the Glen Canyon Group across the reservation. Golden Wingate Sandstone, named for a particularly fine exposure near Fort Wingate, east of Gallup, is topped by red Moenave and Kayenta Formations. The Kayenta contains many tracks of dinosaurs. One of the best-known exposures is west of Tuba City. These siltstones marked the encroachment of interdunal streams before desert conditions returned to western America. Early in the Jurassic, the buff to pink Navajo Sandstone, which forms steep-walled rocky canyons, ledges, alcoves, blind arches, and cliffs ranging from here to Nevada and Wyoming, was laid down in dunes several miles high. The Navajo is 2,000 feet thick in Zion National Park in south-western Utah but thins out considerably on the Navajo reservation.

The sunset-hued Entrada Sandstone is much more evident in the northern reservation. The signature stone of Arches National Park, it forms a white facies—the Cow Springs Sandstone—visible at Window Rock, where erosion has carved a hole in the sandstone behind Navajo Nation headquarters.

Late in the Jurassic, meandering streams and

lakes in low-lying terrain left behind the drab-colored sand- and mudstones of the Morrison Formation. This is a major underlying rock in the Bisti Badlands in the San Juan Basin, where it has produced skeletons of allosaurus, camarasaurus, and other dinosaurs, which were wiped out at the start of the Cenozoic Era, 65 million years ago, ushering in the Age of Mammals.

TREASURE IN THE BASINS

The San Juan and Black Mesa Basins have yielded enormous quantities of coal, oil, and natural gas, much of it laid down during the Cretaceous Period, just prior to the disappearance of the dinosaurs. The Mesa Verde Group, consisting of the Cedar Mountain Formation, Dakota Sandstone, and Mancos Shale, is named for its proximity to the southwestern Colorado national park, where the first oil drilling took place at the Hogback, between Farmington and Shiprock, in the 1920s. Hogbacks, a popular term for the uptilted rocks known as anticlines commonly found along the San Juan River, trap rising petroleum and natural gas close to the surface. In the Black Mesa Basin, it is coal that has brought wealth to towns like Kayenta. Strip-mined by Peabody Corporation atop Black Mesa, south of Monument Valley, coal is mixed with enormous quantities of groundwater to make slurry and piped to Page and Shiprock. Here it is mainly used to generate electricity at the huge Navajo and Four Corners Power Plants.

These forms of energy, the product of decaying plants that died in swamps millions of years ago, have brought enormous wealth to the Navajo Nation in the form of royalties, which have paid for schools, colleges, housing, and other tribal infrastructure. Uranium, first found in the 1950s in the Carrizo Mountains of the Chuska range west of Shiprock, has been a more mixed blessing. Despite the Cold War boom, it has never yielded the big returns enjoyed by coal, oil, and gas. Moreover, it has created a major health risk for thousands of Navajos exposed in mines in the Carrizos and Grants area.

Silver was found by Chief Hoskinnini and his band of Monument Valley Navajos in the mid-1800s, but its precise location has never been disclosed. Two former soldiers in Kit Carson's army, Merrick and Mitchell, returned to Monument Valley after the Long Walk campaign determined to find the mines. According to Louisa Wade Wetherill, daughter of a miner and wife of Oljato Trading Post owner John Wetherill, the men found the silver but never lived to tell the tale. They were killed by Paiutes in Monument Valley beneath the buttes that now carry their name

NAVAJO ORIGINS

The Navajo believe they evolved through four lower worlds, surviving many travails in order to reach this, the Fifth or Glittering World. Epic in scope, the many colorful exploits that make up the Navajo creation story are morality tales, central to Navajo understanding of how they and the world came to be and the daily rituals that still take place on the reservation. There are many different versions of this epic tale. This version comes from Raymond Friday Locke's *The Book of the Navajo*.

THE INSECT PEOPLE

The First World, or Black World, was populated by the Insect People. They lived in dark holes near a stream and had four chiefs—Water Monster, Blue Heron, Frog, and White Mountain Thunder. In time, the Insect People incurred the wrath of their chiefs by quarreling and committing adultery and were banished. A great flood inundated their homes, and they were forced to fly up into the sky, hoping to find an opening. Eventually, they saw one of the Swallow People peering down from above and followed him into the Second World, the Blue World. Here, the Swallow People agreed to allow the refugees to live with them.

Things went well until one of the Insect People seduced the wife of the chief of the Swallow People, and they were banished once more. Flying into the sky, the Insect People found an opening into the Third World, the Yellow World. This was the home of the Grasshopper People, who also agreed to take in the newcomers. But soon enough one of the Insect People had angered their hosts once again by seducing the wife of a chief. This time they were helped by the Red Wind, who told them to fly to the west, where they found a twisted passageway into the Fourth World.

The Fourth World was mixed blue and black. To the East, South, West, and North were four great snow-covered mountains. As they had done in the other worlds, the Insect People sent out the Locusts to investigate this new world. They returned, reporting they had been unable to reach the mountains but had seen the tracks of two animals—Turkey and Deer. In the North, they encountered a race of strange beings who cut their hair square in front, lived in houses, and dry-farmed plots of land. These people—the ancestors of today's Pueblos—invited the Insect People to live among them. By common consent, the Insect People agreed not to anger the Pueblos, and all went well.

FIRST MAN AND FIRST WOMAN

In late autumn, the Insect People were visited by four supernatural beings: White Body, Blue Body, Yellow Body, and Black Body. Using signs, these gods tried to instruct The People but could not be understood. On the fourth day, Black Body reappeared and, speaking to them in their own language, told the Insect People that the gods wished to make new creatures with hands and feet, the first human beings.

The Insect People were ordered to wash. The women then dried themselves with yellow cornmeal and the men dried themselves with white cornmeal. Soon after, the gods appeared again, carrying two buckskins and two ears of corn, one yellow and one white, which they placed on the ground between eagle feathers. Then the wind blew and brought to life the white ear of corn as First Man, and the yellow ear of corn as First Woman. The gods then directed The People to build an enclosure of brushwood, the first hogan, for the pair, where they lived together as husband and wife and gave birth to five pairs of twins.

The gods then took First Man and First Woman and their children to their dwelling place in the East and taught them many things. When they returned, they married among The People, and the descendants of First Man and First Woman invented irrigated farming, pottery, tools, and deer hunting. First Man was chief of all the Dineh. It was he who named the four mountains of the Fourth World—Blanca Peak, San Francisco Peaks, Mount Hesperus, and Mount Taylor—which today mark the boundaries of the Navajo land.

COYOTE BRINGS THE FLOOD

Eight years later, after all of the inhabitants from the lower worlds had evolved into The People of today, they saw the sky and earth join together one day, and from that union arose, first, Coyote, then his brother, Badger. From then on, things began to go wrong in the Fourth World.

First Man and First Woman began to argue about who was most important, and before long, all of the men and women decided to live apart on either side of the river. There they stayed until they agreed to reconcile. All of the women swam across to their husbands, except three, who were seized by Water Monster. Four days later, the gods appeared carrying white and blue shell bowls, which they placed on the river to create an entrance to Water Monster's house. There they found the missing women and brought them home. But unnoticed, Coyote seized two of Water Monster's children and hid them under his big fur robe.

Four days later a great flood arose and all of people and animals in the Fourth World were forced to take refuge in a large, hollow reed. Every individual carried something important, including Turkey, the last to arrive, who brought seeds for planting when they reached the next world. First Man and First Woman sent Great Hawk, Wolf, Coyote, and Lynx to the top of the reed to scratch a hole in the sky. Then Locust flew through the opening to investigate the world above.

When he returned, Locust reported that the Place of Emergence was a small island in the center of a large lake in what is now the San Juan Mountains. The owners of this world were the Grebes. They had challenged him to pass arrows made of the Black Wind through his heart. After he had accomplished this task, the Grebes agreed to leave. First Man and First Woman then asked Badger to enlarge the hole into the Fifth World with his claws. When Badger returned his legs were stained black with mud, a characteristic of all badgers ever since. Everyone then climbed through into the Fifth World, the present world of the Five-Fingered People, the Dineh.

Blue Body appeared and, with the help of the Smooth Wind, helped The People drain the lake so that they could reach land. Here, the Pueblos built shelters of mud and stone and The People built shelters of brushwood, as they do today. Coyote then threw a stone into the water to divine if The People would live or die. When it sank, The People agreed that some should leave in order to make room for others, and so the concept of Death was introduced. Soon after, one of the children of First Man and First Woman died and was laid to rest. But one man looked down at the deceased and died soon after. From then on, the Dineh feared to look upon the dead in case they should die themselves.

Coyote could be wise, but he was also lazy and played tricks. He grabbed the blanket on which First Man and First Woman were placing bright lights and threw them into the air, creating the first stars. And when flood waters continued to pour into the Fifth World, The People found out that Coyote was to blame for stealing Water Monster's children. Angry, they returned the babies to the Fourth World and the floodwaters no longer inundated the Fifth World.

THE GLITTERING WORLD

First Man and First Woman, Black Body and Blue Body left The People and built seven sacred mountains. Four peaks resembled the mountains of the East, South, West, and North from the Fourth World. Within that circle, they also created two other sacred peaks: Gobernador Peak and Huerfano Mesa. But all was not well. During their separation in the Fourth World, the wives of the Dineh had committed unnatural sexual acts and began to give birth to monsters who roamed the countryside killing and eating The People. To help them, the Holy People journeyed to Huerfano Mesa and created Ever Changing Woman and White Shell Woman. The sisters lay down beneath the Sun and the Waterfall and soon gave birth to twin boys, Monster Slayer and Child Born for Water, who grew to adulthood within four days.

Witnessing the terrible suffering in their homeland, the boys decided to visit their father, the Sun, to see if he could help them rid *Dine Bikeyah* of these monsters. They were shown the way by Spider Woman who gave them a charm to protect them and taught them to use sacred pollen to bring peace to their enemies. After a long and dangerous journey, they reached the house of the Sun, in the West. He gave them special clothing, arrows, and knives to kill the monsters. The Hero Twins then returned home and eventually killed all the monsters so that the Dineh could live in peace. You can still see the petrified bodies of the monsters today, dotted throughout the Navajo reservation, where they serve as constant reminders of the heroic past of the Navajo people in reaching their homeland.

THE NAVAJO RESERVATION

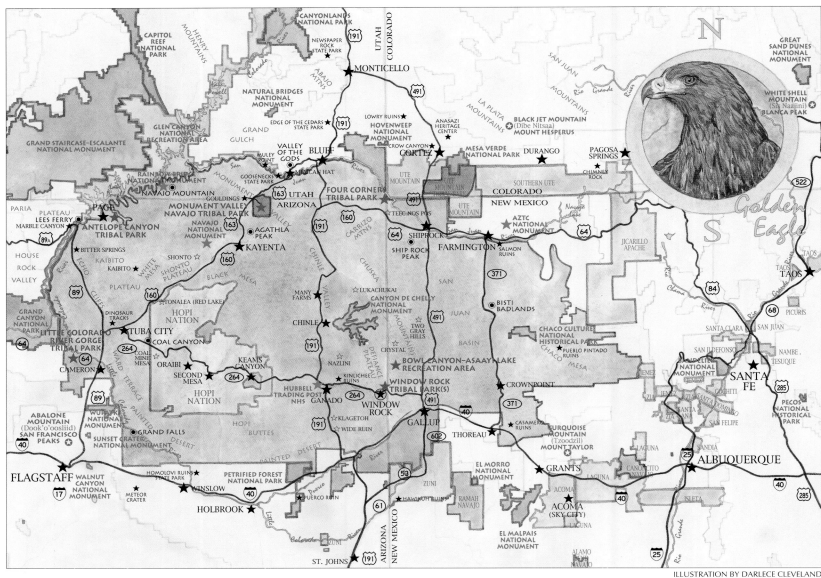

ILLUSTRATION BY DARLECE CLEVELAND

At 29,817 square miles, the Navajo reservation, also known as the Navajo Nation or *Dine Bikeyah*, the homeland of the Dineh, is a remarkable place. Larger than the state of West Virginia, it spans redrock mesas, black lava promontories, mountain ranges, and two huge mountain basins, covering northwestern New Mexico, northeastern Arizona, and southeastern Utah. The original 1868 reservation encompasses either side of the Chuska Mountains on the Arizona–New Mexico border. As the tribe's population rebounded, federal appropriations and tribal acquisitions were used to purchase badly needed new lands for homesites and grazing livestock.

Constant expansion has created odd boundaries on the Big Rez. In Arizona, the Navajo Nation entirely surrounds the tiny Hopi reservation, which has led to an ongoing land dispute, with serious consequences for people of both tribes living in Joint Use Areas. On the eastern side of the reservation is the Checkerboard, a patchwork

of public-private ownership. Between Gallup and Albuquerque, south of I-40, are three small Navajo communities: the Ramah chapter, just east of Zuni Pueblo; the Alamo chapter, north of Magdalena; and the Canoncito chapter, west of Albuquerque. The northeastern San Juan Basin— an area called the Dinetah, where the Navajo first lived after arriving from the northwest—is also checkerboard. It surrounds Chaco Cultural National Historical Park and includes US 550 as far as the San Juan Mountains on the Colorado border.

The Navajo are a sovereign nation, but their lands are held in trust by the U.S. government. After Navajo leaders signed the 1868 treaty allowing them to return to their homeland, agents of the Bureau of Indian Affairs were sent to Fort Defiance to set up the promised new schools, hospitals, monthly rations, and political infrastructure to help the tribe get back on its feet. The seeds of the tribe's independence were sown in 1923 when the government set up

the Navajo Nation Tribal Council to negotiate oil, and later natural gas, coal, and uranium, lease payments to the tribe after huge reserves were found beneath the reservation. Since the 1950s, money from these leases has been reinvested in infrastructure that benefits the whole tribe. The Navajo now operate their own police force, hospitals, schools, colleges, housing department, museums, arts cooperatives, parks and recreation, archaeological sites, tribal forests, and other natural resources. Tribal headquarters is at Window Rock, centrally located on the Arizona– New Mexico border.

The tribal council was reorganized in 1991 and now includes 110 chapters, or local councils, represented by 88 delegates at Window Rock, the capital of the Navajo Nation. The chapter houses offer a place where the people can be heard by their representatives. They also function as important community centers, often the only connection isolated families have with the rest of the reservation.

OPPOSITE: Three Sisters, West Mitten, and Big Chief as seen from near Rabbit and Stagecoach, Monument Valley. PHOTO ©WILLARD CLAY

The San Francisco Peaks (Abalone Mountain), north of Flagstaff, Arizona.

PHOTO ©TOM BROWNOLD

THE SACRED PEAKS

A traditional Navajo will never travel far from the circle of four sacred mountains that mark the boundaries of the Navajo world. According to the Navajo creation story, each of the volcanic peaks—one for every compass direction—was created by First Man and First Woman, assisted by Black Body and Blue Body.

Blanca Peak, *Sis Naajini*, or White Shell Mountain, is located near Alamosa, Colorado. It is the sacred mountain of the East, an important direction since it represents the direction from which the Holy People came to instruct the Five-Fingered People in how to live in this, the Fifth or Glittering World. Rock Crystal Boy and Rock Crystal Girl were placed on Blanca Peak to serve as its guardians. First Man and First Woman fastened down the mountain with lightning, populated it with Pigeon and other animals, and adorned it with white shell, white corn, and dark clouds that would produce the hard "male" rains of summer.

Mount Taylor, *Tzoodzil*, also known as Turquoise Mountain, is located east of Grants, New Mexico. It is the sacred mountain of the South. First Man and First Woman set the mountain in place with a great stone knife and decorated it with turquoise, Blue Bird and other animals, and gave it dark mist to produce the gentle "female" rains of spring. Then they covered it with blue sky and placed Boy Who is Bringing Back Turquoise and Girl Who is Bringing Back Many Ears of Corn to protect it.

The San Francisco Peaks, *Dook' o' oosliid*, also known as Abalone Mountain, is located north of Flagstaff, Arizona. It is the sacred mountain of the West. First Man and First Woman fastened it with a sunbeam and decorated the summit with abalone shell. They placed Yellow Warbler and many other animals there and created White Corn Boy and Yellow Corn Girl to be its guardians. They shrouded the mountain with a dark cloud to produce heavy "male" rains and covered all of this with a yellow cloud.

Mount Hesperus, *Dibe Nitsaa*, or Black Jet Mountain, is in the La Plata Mountains of southwestern Colorado. It is the sacred mountain of the North. First Man and First Woman secured the mountain with a rainbow and adorned it with black beads of jet. Many animals were placed on it, including Black Bird, and Pollen Boy and Grasshopper Girl were sent to guard it. The peak was covered with gray clouds that produce the gentle "female" rains and then shrouded in darkness. In Navajo belief, North is the direction of darkness and death. If a Navajo dies prematurely or under strange circumstances, the door and smoke hole of their hogan are sealed and the north wall broken out to let the ghost, or *chiidee*, of the dead person escape to the north.

OPPOSITE: Star-trails in early morning sky above The Mittens, Monument Valley. PHOTO ©KERRICK JAMES

Navajos in Canyon de Chelly, circa 1904.

KIT CARSON AND THE LONG WALK

In 1864, Fort Sumner in eastern New Mexico became the first concentration camp on American soil. Although it was officially called an Indian "reservation," for the more than 9,000 Navajos forced to live there, it was a living hell of starvation, illness, and death. Elders said The People had brought this bad luck on themselves by falling out of harmony with the Holy People's teachings. No one, however, could have predicted the suffering The People would have to endure before they could return to their homeland.

In the fall of 1863, Lieutenant Kit Carson, under orders from General Carleton, undertook a "scorched earth" campaign to subdue the Navajo. Focusing on Canyon de Chelly, Carson and his men slaughtered livestock, destroyed peach trees and cornfields, and burned hogans. Faced with starvation, thousands began to surrender at Fort Defiance. Some bands, however, managed to escape to remote areas of Navajo Country, such as Monument Valley and the Grand Canyon, where they hid from the soldiers.

Ragged and weakened by hunger, men, women, and children journeyed on foot in the dead of winter to Bosque Redondo in New Mexico, 300 miles away. Many died on the Long Walk, were shot for lagging behind, or were seized by New Mexicans as slaves. Conditions at Fort Sumner were no better. Families were forced to live in holes in the ground or makeshift shelters made of wood collected from miles away. The river water was brackish and caused dysentery. The remaining livestock died or was seized by Comanche raiders. Crops would not grow in the poor, alkaline soil. Worse still, the army was too short of rations, at the height of the Civil War, to adequately feed them.

A public outcry led to the release of the Navajo in 1868. Barboncito, the "Peace Chief," was the first of 12 headmen to sign the treaty that created the new 6,120-square-mile Navajo reservation. Families were given 160 acres to farm, $100 in farming equipment and seed, and 15,000 sheep and 500 cattle were divided among them. Children between the ages of 6 and 16 were required to attend school.

But the Navajo returned to their homeland a changed people. After years of living on army rations, they now prized canned peaches, Bluebird flour (milled at nearby Cortez, Colorado), Arbuckle coffee, and other white-man's foods in addition to their mutton stews. The women adapted the clothing they saw army wives wearing into velveteen blouses and flounced broomstick skirts. These necessities were provided to them at newly established trading posts on the reservation. In the years to come, trusted traders like Lorenzo Hubbell and C. N. Cotton would be a lifeline for the Navajo, helping them survive by exchanging blankets, rugs, silver jewelry, and other crafts for food, cloth, and other necessities.

OPPOSITE: Canyon de Chelly as seen from near Tsegi Overlook, Canyon de Chelly National Monument. PHOTO ©RANDY PRENTICE

MONUMENT VALLEY

Churro sheep at North Window, Monument Valley.   PHOTO ©RICHARD D. STRANGE

Susie Yazzie is sitting on a sheepskin in her hogan, demonstrating how she prepares wool for weaving. She is dressed in a velveteen blouse, flowing broomstick skirt, and tennis shoes. Her soft, smiling face and supple hands are brown and lined from countless summers in the sun. Her long silver hair is bundled into a traditional bun fastened with white cotton cord. A heavy turquoise-and-silver squash blossom necklace hangs around her neck. Tables on either side of the room display photos and magazine articles about Susie. As a young woman, she appeared in John Ford movies and many photographs by Josef Muench. In the 1930s, Muench helped trader Harry Goulding publicize Monument Valley in Hollywood. Today, thousands of people have met Susie on a backcountry tour. She is one of Monument Valley's best-known residents.

Hands slapping back on forth, she cards the gray-brown matted wool from her hardy Spanish *churro* sheep between two combed paddles and fluffs the long, lanolin-rich fibers into small bundles. Then she pinches part of a bundle, smooths it between a practiced forefinger and thumb, winds it onto an old-fashioned spindle, and begins expertly spinning long strands of wool. Once she has enough, she will dye it into subtle shades of ochre, taupe, lavender, and rose, using dyes made from plants growing nearby. When it is dry, she will wind each skein into balls, ready for weaving, with the help of her great-grandchildren who have come to visit this Easter day.

Now in her early 90s, Susie's eyesight is beginning to fail and her hand reflexively massages one arthritic leg, but her mind is as sharp as that of someone many decades younger. Her good health, she tells me, comes from rising before dawn each day to greet the Holy People in the east, then walking around her property to check on her sheep and goats, corralled beneath a mesa overhang. Like other traditional Navajo, Susie strives for *hozhoo*, a state of being in harmony with all things, and considers most problems result from falling out of balance with the teachings of the Holy People.

Following our guide's instructions, we enter her hogan clockwise from the door on the east and offer her a soft handshake and a tentative *ya-ah-teeh* (hello) in Navajo, then squat on either side of her in silence. She agrees to pose for a photographer's camera for a small additional fee, eyes downcast in the modest Navajo way. Then she turns toward her upright loom—its healds firmly set into the packed earth of the floor—and weaves part of her latest rug, a design featuring *yeibichei*, the gods invoked in Navajo dances.

Susie Yazzie's homestead sits between Raingod and Thunderbird Mesas on a potholed backcountry trail deep within Monument Valley, the place known to the Navajo as *Tse' Bii' Ndzisgaii*, "valley between the rocks." Our guide on this trip is Daniel Begay, an affable Navajo in his forties who lives with his family in a hogan just north of Monument Valley. During our two-and-a-half-hour tour in a small open Jeep (Navajos call their cars "chitties"), Daniel points out the landmarks of Monument Valley and recounts stories about each one. It's a time-honored tradition here to learn the stories associated with a particular locale and to put your own stamp on them for dramatic effect. Daniel is no exception. As we pass each landmark, he tells us their popular names and encourages us to look closer. Can we make out an Indian chief in this rock? Do we notice this one looks like a bear? Do we see an eagle in flight in this alcove?

Daniel's own story is interesting. He was born at a Mormon mission in nearby Bluff, Utah, and sent away to live with a family in Las Vegas, Nevada, during the school year. On holidays, he returned home to help his family with herding and other chores. After graduation, he stayed in Las Vegas and worked for his other family's construction company. A year and a half ago, he returned to Monument Valley, pulled back like many Navajo to a lifestyle he missed. He speaks only a little Navajo and is avidly learning more about his own culture to share with others.

Daniel was born into the Red House and Edgewater clans. One's clan affiliations are a basic part of what it means to be Navajo, recalling a time when family bands of Navajo lived a more nomadic existence and depended on each other for support. The first Navajo clans date back to The People's arrival in the Dinetah and were named for important characteristics associated with their territory, such

---

Classic view of The Mittens as seen from Lookout Point, Monument Valley.

as the Bitter Water People and the Mud People. As Mexicans, Apaches, and other groups joined the Dineh, new clans were created. There are more than one hundred today. Marriage within one's own clan is forbidden. Even more important is loyalty. Family members still set great store in helping one another, no matter how hard the task. There are no orphans in a Navajo clan.

Towards the end of our trip, we stop to view rock art and homes left behind by the people the Navajo call the Anasazi, the Ancient Ones, who lived here a thousand years ago. In the western area of the valley are tiny one-room pueblos and granaries secreted beneath overhangs. Nearby we see many well-preserved panels of rock art. Some are quite unusual and include recumbent Kokopellis, the famous flute players found throughout the Southwest. There are many more Ancestral Pueblo dwellings in Mystery Valley, on the other side of Wetherill Mesa. These silent stone houses can be found all across the Navajo reservation, a place where past and present dwell side by side and people keep a respectful distance for fear of disturbing the spirits of those who came before.

Square House Ruin, Mystery Valley, sunset.

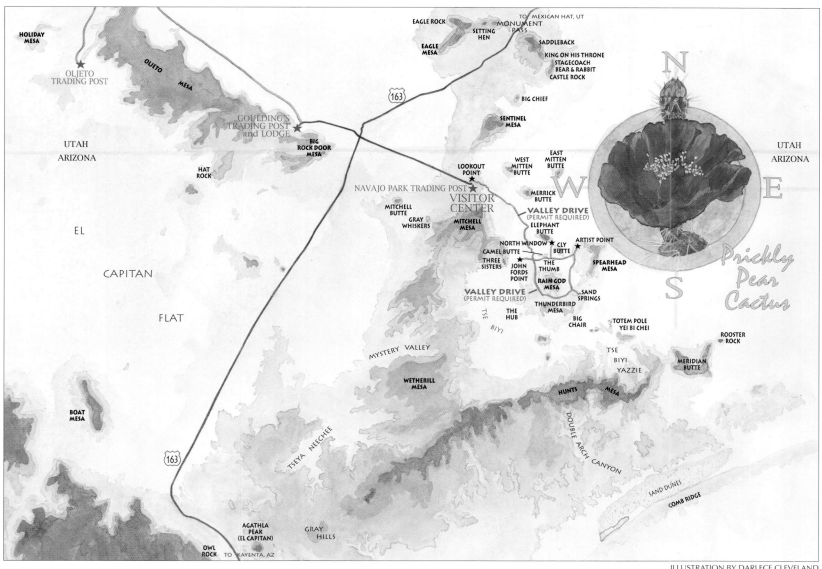

ILLUSTRATION BY DARLECE CLEVELAND

Monument Valley Navajo Tribal Park is located off US 163, 20 miles north of Kayenta, Arizona. The park was set aside in 1958 to preserve 50 square miles of sandstone buttes, mesas, spires, and arches; more than 100 Ancestral Pueblo remains; and living examples of Navajo culture. The dozen or so families who live in Monument Valley view it as a giant sacred hogan, with Oljato Mesa, near Gouldings Lodge, as the fireplace, the ranger station as the east-facing door, and Sentinel Mesa and Gray Whiskers Mesa as the doorposts. The Mittens are believed to be hands left behind by the Holy People to signal that one day they will rule again. Eagle Mesa is especially sacred, for it is here that the spirit of the dead person goes after burial. Totem Pole and the neighboring Yeibichei formation are said to be a line of prayer sticks, or petrified *yei*, held up by lightning.

Begin a visit to Monument Valley at the visitor cen-

ter, which has exhibits about the Dineh way of life, restrooms, and water. Food is available daily in The View Restaurant. Navajo Park Trading Post sells Navajo arts and crafts, books, and other gifts. Allow at least two hours to tour the 17-mile-long, unpaved scenic drive into the valley. The dusty, rutted road may be driven by passenger cars but becomes impassable after rain. Inquire before setting out. Be sure to bring plenty of water and food with you. These are not available along the tour route.

A tour booklet offers information on 11 scenic overlooks along the drive, including John Ford Point, made famous by the director of legendary Westerns such as *Stagecoach, Cheyenne,* and *She Wore a Yellow Ribbon.* Sand Springs, Monument Valley's only water source, offers glimpses of a hogan, corrals, sheep and goats, and local residents dressed in traditional clothing. **Note:** Offroad hiking, biking, camping, horseback riding, and four-wheel-

driving are only allowed with a registered Navajo guide. A number of professionally run companies offer reasonably priced tours daily. Sign-up booths are located at the visitor center, nearby Gouldings Lodge, and in Kayenta. Cash only, unless you book ahead.

For further information, write Monument Valley Navajo Tribal Park, P.O. Box 360289, Monument Valley, UT 84536; (435) 727-5870, or contact Navajo Parks and Recreation Dept., P.O. Box 9000, Window Rock, AZ 86515; (520) 871-6647. Monument Valley Visitor Center is open daily, except Christmas Day. May-Sept. 8 a.m.–7 p.m.; winter: 8 a.m.–5 p.m. **Note:** the Navajo Nation observes Daylight Savings Time April-Oct., an hour ahead of nearby Arizona locations.

Buttes and mesas of Monument Valley as seen from John Ford Point.

JOHN FORD AND THE MOVIES ARRIVE

Legendary Hollywood film director John Ford—winner of a record six Oscars—set nine of his Westerns in Monument Valley. *She Wore a Yellow Ribbon* (1949), *The Searchers* (1956), *Sergeant Rutledge* (1960), *Cheyenne Autumn* (1964), and other films used many famous rocks in the valley as a backdrop, including The Mittens, the Yeibichei, Three Sisters, and Sand Springs. The view to the north will be familiar to movie-goers the world over—two landmarks are named for the famed director and his work: John Ford Point and Stagecoach Mesa.

Ford's first film in Monument Valley was 1939's *Stagecoach*, the colorful story of a west-bound stagecoach and its passengers. Still considered a perfect Western today, *Stagecoach* made a star of a hard-working, young B movie actor named John Wayne. The Duke's good looks, lanky frame, and courtly manners perfectly evoked the rugged loner beloved in classic novels of the American West such as Owen Wister's *The Virginian*. Wayne was eventually named one of the top three most popular actors of all time.

Wayne and Ford were perfectly matched. Ford, the son of an Irish saloon keeper from Maine, fell in love with the mythical American West at an early age. *Stagecoach* was based on characters in an Ernest Haycox short story called "Stage to Lordsburg," itself a 20th-century adaptation of 19th-century French short-story writer Guy de Maupassant's classic tale *"Boule de Suif"* ("Ball of

Fat"). Ford drew heavily on the work of Western artist Frederic Remington for the look of *Stagecoach* and *She Wore a Yellow Ribbon*.

Monument Valley's popularity with Hollywood was the result of the hard work of one man: Harry Goulding. Colorado-raised Goulding and his new wife "Mike" arrived in Monument Valley in 1923 and immediately embraced the area. They bought 640 acres of former Paiute land, pitched a tent, and began trading with the Dineh out of the back of a horse-drawn wagon. In the 1930s, they built a stone trading post and house and went into the hospitality business, publicizing the area to famous Hollywood directors like Ford and others. Known as an honest trader by the Dineh, who dubbed him "Long Sheep," Goulding (along with traders John and Marietta Wetherill who had run a post at Oljato) named many of Monument Valley's landmarks.

Goulding's original trading post, adjoining the modern Gouldings motel complex, is now a delightful museum. On the first floor, the trading post is much as Mike Goulding left it when she died in the 1990s. The second floor is given over to movie stills and memorabilia from movies shot in Monument Valley, including Ford's work and more recent movies, such as *2001: A Space Odyssey, Forrest Gump*, and *Back to the Future*. The cabin used by John Wayne in *She Wore a Yellow Ribbon* can be seen behind the post.

OPPOSITE: Buttes of Monument Valley seen from Sand Springs Dunes. PHOTO ©TOM TILL

ANCIENT ENEMIES

Bighorn sheep petroglyph near God's Eye, Monument Valley.   PHOTO ©BRUCE HUCKO

Anasazi, they are called by the Dineh. It's a word that, in the complex Navajo language, means several different things. Ancient Tribe. Ancient Enemies. Enemy Ancestors. Those Who Came Before. Even, according to one source, People Who Left Their Granaries Behind. While officials vacillate over whether to call the forebears of modern Pueblo people by the politically neutral but awkward term "Ancestral Puebloans," the Dineh stand firm. For them, the ancient stone-city builders they encountered in the Southwest centuries ago remain *Anasazi*—the ancestors of a respected culture whose history is intertwined with their own.

The Navajo live alongside thousands of Anasazi pithouses and *pueblos,* or villages. With their fear of *chiidi*, or ghosts of the dead, few traditional Navajos enter such places; those who do—almost without exception—engage in purification rituals. However, it is common to find homesteads that have been used by generations of Navajo farmers located very close to former Anasazi dwellings and walls of rock art. These ancient sites are usually near rivers and streams with fertile bottomlands and irrigation water. In the drought-ridden Southwest, both are essential for growing corn and other crops.

The Dineh not only learned farming from the Pueblos but also the importance of spreading impacts seasonally across a larger land base: planting and nurturing crops in spring and summer, harvesting and drying crops in early fall, hunting in late fall and early winter, and gathering wild plants throughout the year to supplement their diet. Pueblos and Dineh engaged in trading and intermarriage during times of peace. Both peoples practiced pottery making and weaving with cotton, the latter a skill at which the Navajo, using Spanish wool, would soon excel.

In the years after the 1680 Pueblo Revolt, refugees from the 19 Rio Grande Pueblos joined the Navajo in the Dinetah. Some also traveled west to northern Arizona, where they were taken in by the Hopi pueblos, which had fought fiercely to maintain their independence from Spanish rule. From this time on, Pueblo and Navajo cultural history grew increasingly intertwined. According to oral traditions, the Navajo met the *kisani*, as Pueblos are called, in the Fourth World and learned farming from them there. The two cultures arrived in the Fifth World together, then spread apart, with the Pueblos living in stone villages and the Navajo living in their circular hogans.

The difference in living arrangements is one of the most important distinguishing factors between the Navajo and Pueblo cultures. While the Navajo are still seminomadic—often moving between two and three homes throughout the year—Pueblos, as their name suggests, are most comfortable living in villages. It wasn't always that way. For much of their early history, Anasazi families lived in scattered pithouses. These semicircular, high-desert dugouts had earthen roofs held up by sturdy tree trunks and were cool in summer and snug in winter. For many, they remained the dwelling of choice—an architectural form that would never fully be abandoned.

By the 700s, the Anasazi had fully embraced farming, a labor-intensive way of life that required greater cooperation than hunting and gathering. Families joined together and built compounds of simple, above-ground houses around small communal plazas, using shaped stones mortared and plastered with mud. Strong *viga* roof beams of ponderosa pine interwoven with *latillas* of juniper and aspen poles could support more than one story, allowing buildings to grow as needed with new residential and storage rooms. Pithouses were incorporated into the pueblos as underground ceremonial rooms called *kivas*. They were used by clansmen to plan crop ceremonies, discuss politics, weave cotton, and work turquoise.

Beginning in the 10th century, Anasazi civilization exploded throughout the Four Corners. It began in remote Chaco Canyon in northwestern New Mexico. Chaco's central location in the 25,000-square-mile San Juan Basin may have been the key to its success. Its leaders seem to have been politically savvy priests who monitored the skies and controlled seasonal agricultural ceremonies across a vast

Kivas within the walls of Pueblo Bonito, Chaco Canyon.

area. Evidence suggests this elite resided in specially built apartments within enormous public complexes known as Great Houses. Pilgrims from throughout the region met several times a year to trade, take part in ceremonies in Great Kivas, and perhaps fulfill work requirements. Chaco may have served as an important redistribution center for food and goods as the climate became more unstable in the 11th century.

Everything fell apart spectacularly in the mid-1100s, when a long-running drought tipped the balance. Chacoans fled the canyon. The leaders may have started over at nearby outliers such as Aztec and Salmon Pueblos, situated along the San Juan and Animas Rivers. Others walked as far as the Jemez Mountains and made new communities in what is now Bandelier National Monument. Others moved to the Kayenta area of northern Arizona and built homes in canyons on the Defiance Plateau carved by the Rio de Chelly. And still others joined people living in the foothills of the San Juan Mountains along the Colorado–Utah border, creating a new center of political power centered on a well-watered highland known as Mesa Verde.

By the 1200s, people throughout the Southwest were building carefully hidden homes in cliff alcoves. These defensive homes suggest the Anasazi may have been plagued by problems—perhaps raiding, perhaps internal strife. Or they may simply have found the sandstone alcoves with their dripping springs a practical solution to cramped living arrangements brought about by an influx of newcomers. Finally, the Great Drought of 1276–1299 drove people out of the Four Corners. They joined other Pueblos along the Rio Grande and its tributaries and atop the Hopi Mesas near the Little Colorado River in northern Arizona, where their descendants live today.

Aerial view of Acoma Pueblo (Sky City), one of the oldest continuously occupied villages in the New World.

HOPI AND PUEBLO

The *Hopitu*, the "peaceful people," are the descendants of the Anasazi, whom they call *Hisatsinom*. They live a very different kind of life from their Navajo neighbors, whose much larger reservation completely surrounds theirs. The 12 east-facing Hopi villages atop three windswept mesas in northern Arizona have changed little since late Pueblo times. Hopi men dry-farm untilled plots of corn, melons, squash, and other crops at the base of the cliffs and in terraces that catch the scant 10 inches of rain that fall here each year.

According to oral histories, the Bear Clan was the first to arrive on the mesas in the 12th century. In time, other clans migrated from nearby Wupatki, Walnut Canyon, Homolovi, and other drought-ridden pueblos. Each was asked to contribute a different skill or ceremony to ensure the well-being of people on earth. From this, a complex seasonal ceremonial calendar was devised, with sun priests in each village determining the timing of ceremonies based on the positions of the sun, moon, and planets.

The most important Hopi ceremony of the year is the Niman, or Home Dance, in July, when the *kachinas*—serving as supernatural intermediaries between the Creator Spirit and the people of Earth—return to their winter home in the San Francisco Peaks after blessing the crops and bringing rain. The hypnotic dancing and singing of the kachinas symbolize the harmony of good thought and deed necessary for a balanced life and to bring the blessing of rain.

Information on current dances is available at the Hopi Cultural Center on Second Mesa. Displays introduce you to the culture of the Hopi and the specialized crafts on each mesa. First Mesa is known for its pottery. Second and Third Mesas are renowned for their basketry. Kachina dolls and silversmiths work on all the mesas. The cultural center offers tours that include workshops, craft stores, villags, and other places of interest. The villages of Shungapovi, Shipaulovi, and Mishongnovi all feature dances.

New Mexico's 19 modern pueblos are mostly located along the Rio Grande and its tributaries. After their ancestors migrated from the Four Corners to the Rio Grande, New Mexico's pueblos—as at Hopi—became large, self-contained entities specializing in superb arts and crafts for trade. Acoma, Zuni, Laguna, Zia, and Santa Ana make beautiful black-on-white and polychrome ceramics; San Ildefonso and Santa Clara specialize in polished red and black pots; Picuris and Taos make glittering micaceous pottery; and Tesuque and Cochiti potters create unusual ceramic figurines. Santo Domingo is known for its worked turquoise *heishi* (disks) necklaces and other jewelry. Taos and Picuris, heavily influenced by their proximity to the Plains, make drums and leather goods.

For more information, visit Albuquerque's excellent Pueblo Indian Cultural Center or the Eight Northern Pueblos Cultural Center at San Juan Pueblo, just north of Espanola.

The walls of Hungo Pavi and distant Fajada Butte, Chaco Canyon, New Mexico.

PHOTO ©TOM TILL

"It was the very symbol of Pueblo civilization in full flower," said archaeologist Neil Judd of Chaco Canyon. Judd's excavations for the Smithsonian Institution during the 1920s focused on Pueblo Bonito, the largest of the multilevel public buildings. First excavated between 1896 and 1899 by cowboy-archaeologist Richard Wetherill—who, following the lead of his Navajo workers, gave the name "Anasazi" to the Pueblos—the three-acre, D-shaped Great House of Pueblo Bonito stunned all who saw it. It rose five stories in back and had 650 rooms around an enclosed plaza dotted with three Great Kivas and more than 30 small kivas. Begun in A.D. 950, the pueblo had grown to its present size through the toil of generations of workers directed by Chaco's leaders: a priestly elite whose power derived from their knowledge of astronomy, ritual, and social organization.

Inside, archaeologists uncovered huge quantities of black-on-white pottery, raw and worked turquoise, carved effigies inlaid with precious stones, Pacific shells, Mexi-can copper bells, colorful macaw feathers and bones, and 375 carved wooden ceremonial staffs. Even today, Chaco's high, tapering walls are distinctive. Core-and-veneer construction, a technique in which two walls several feet apart are filled with rubble and mortar, made them strong. Artistry made them beautiful. Chacoan masons laid dressed sandstone tablets in courses and tightly chinked them with smaller stones; yet mud plaster and paint hid the whole thing.

To date, the National Park Service's Chaco Project has located more than 3,600 archaeological sites in Chaco Canyon and the surrounding area, along with a 400-mile road system connecting Chaco to satellite villages, or outliers. Every piece of timber (carried here from mountain forests as far away as 30-60 miles) has been dated. It's now known that Pueblo Bonito and the clifftop pueblo of Penasco Blanco were begun earlier than first thought. Their construction coincided with a particularly wet period in the Southwest, leading archaeologists to theorize that Chaco's importance as a ceremonial center arose from its central location in an agricultural area.

Plan a trip to this remote canyon carefully. The main park turnoff, just south of Nageezi, on US 550, crosses 21 miles of the Navajo reservation on an unpaved, washboarded road. You'll need to bring all your own food, beverages, gas, and camping gear; none are available at the park. The main ruins sit on a nine-mile loop, west of the visitor center. On the north side are Chetro Ketl, Pueblo Bonito, Pueblo del Arroyo, and a trail leading to two 12th-century Mesa Verde–style pueblos: Casa Chiquita and Kin Kletso. South of Chaco Wash is the Great Kiva of Casa Rinconada and several small village sites. Backcountry trails lead up to the 300-foot-high cliffs to Pueblo Alto, Tsin Kletsin, Wijiji, and Penasco Blanco, and several important rock art sites. These are accessible on foot only, with a permit available from the visitor center.

OPPOSITE: Kivas and walls of Pueblo Bonito, winter, Chaco Canyon. PHOTO ©GEORGE H. H. HUEY

Hogan on the floor of Canyon de Chelly near 800-foot Spider Rock.   PHOTO ©RANDY PRENTICE

Few places on the Navajo reservation are as important to the Navajo as 130-square-mile Canyon de Chelly (pronounced *de shay*) National Monument in northern Arizona. Here in this lovely canyon—and its equally pretty tributary, Canyon del Muerto—the colorful traditions of the Dineh are vividly on display. Hogans, livestock corrals, peach trees, and carefully tended fields of corn form attractive homesteads deep inside the canyons. Women weave rugs under shade ramadas. Children play ball on the banks of the shallow Rio de Chelly. Pickups filled with family members bump over the sandy canyon bottom. Their shouts bounce off the 1,000-foot-high cliffs of ruddy de Chelly Sandstone to the rims, where visitors at overlooks along the 35-mile-long South and North Rim Drives watch with delight.

The sights and sounds of this living culture stand in stark contrast to the now-silent former homes of their predecessors, the Anasazi. More than 700 prehistoric ruins have been found in the canyons, representing a thousand years of occupation. Most dramatic are the south-facing, multistoried cliff pueblos of Antelope House, Mummy Cave Ruin, Junction Ruin, White House, and other cliff dwellings constructed between the 11th and 13th centuries in alcoves high above the canyon floor. It's still unclear why they were built in these inaccessible locations. Drought? Flooding? To deter raiders? Whatever the reason, by A.D. 1300, the Anasazi had moved away. It's likely they moved to the Hopi Mesas. In the centuries that followed, Hopi farmers used these canyons seasonally, later planting peach trees they obtained from the Spanish.

In the 1700s, Navajo fugitives evaded Spanish reprisals for persistent attacks on Rio Grande villages by hiding in the canyon. Massacre Cave in Canyon del Muerto is the site of the 1805 Spanish attack that left 115 Navajos dead. For the Navajo, the dark shadow of the 1864 Long Walk still hangs heavy over Canyon de Chelly. Kit Carson's "scorched earth" campaign very nearly succeeded in destroying the Dineh way of life. On September 9, 1849, they had signed a peace treaty on the south rim of Canyon de Chelly acknowledging United States rule, only to see the fragile peace degenerate into war, subjugation, and incarceration, before they were allowed to return to their homeland in 1868.

The 1849 treaty site is now the visitor center for the national monument, unique in the national park system because it is entirely owned by the Navajo Nation. Because Navajos live in the canyons and on the rim, entry into the canyons is restricted to a steep, 2.5-mile trail leading to White House Ruin. If you have your own four-wheel-drive vehicle, consider hiring a Navajo guide. Tours take in major pueblos and rock art sites, as well as Spider Rock, the mythical home of Spider Woman, one of the Holy People. Concessionaires based at the attractive 1902 Thunderbird Lodge also offer half- and full-day tours in large, jostling, open-air vehicles dubbed "shake-and-bakes."

OPPOSITE: White House Ruin in its incomparable setting, Canyon de Chelly. PHOTO ©LARRY ULRICH

The view from deep inside Keet Seel, Navajo National Monument.   PHOTO ©GARY LADD

The half-mile-long Sandal Trail winds gently from behind the visitor center at 360-acre Navajo National Monument to its terminus above Tsegi Canyon (Navajo for "Rock Canyon"). At first, the 450-foot-high alcove across from the overlook seems like any other break in the canyon wall created by the relentless dripping of water through porous pink sandstone. Then the eyes adjust and you see it: a 135-room pueblo harmonizing so well with its surroundings it hides in plain sight.

Betatakin (Navajo for "Ledge House") was built by people of the Kayenta Anasazi culture from the surrounding Tsegi Canyon–Marsh Pass area. Perhaps due to drought, a few adventurous families moved here in A.D. 1250 and stockpiled timber for construction. They were joined by a large group of settlers in 1275, who worked with them to construct the pueblo. Kayenta Anasazi architecture—with its large stones and abundant use of mud mortar—was serviceable, displaying none of the virtuos-ity of earlier Chaco masons. However, this pueblo's location in a protected alcove has helped make it one of the best-preserved pueblos in the Southwest.

Betatakin has several unusual features. Due to the sloping bedrock floor of the cave, the pueblo had to be supported on a foundation of "wall-footing grooves" and shored up with mud for greater stability. A retaining wall was built, behind which graded earth provided a level walkway for residents. Rock art here includes bighorn sheep, as well as the Hopi Fire Clan symbol, leading some Hopis to claim this as an ancestral site; they call it *Kawestima*, or "North Village."

A second, larger pueblo, Keet Seel, lies eight miles in the backcountry and requires a permit and challenging overnight hike to view. Keet Seel was originally founded in A.D. 950 by groups whose homes were probably destroyed by the later "Tsegi Phase" builders who contructed this pueblo in 1250, reusing timbers from earlier residences.

The estimated 150 people who lived at Keet Seel in its heyday were more mobile than the people of Betatakin, as reflected in the wide range of influences felt in their architecture here.

Scheduled five-mile, ranger-led hikes to Betatakin are offered each morning in summer and are limited to 25 hikers. To avoid disappointment, stay in the monument's delightful 30-site campground and get to the visitor center early in the morning to obtain a ticket for the hike. The ranger-led, 17-mile hike to Keet Seel is limited to 20 visitors; make reservations well in advance and be sure you're in good shape and well equipped before setting out. Charming Navajo National Monument is located on the Shonto Plateau and is one of the area's least-known parks. It is 28 miles west of Kayenta, at the end of a 10-mile-long, paved road, and is free and open year round.

OPPOSITE: The amazing village of Betatakin in Tsegi Canyon, Navajo National Monument. PHOTO ©GEORGE H. H. HUEY

TOURING THE RESERVATION

Highway 163 approaching Monument Valley from the northeast. PHOTO ©DICK DIETRICH

A visit to the vast Navajo Nation can begin anywhere. Your best bet is to use one of the small outlying cities that serve as commercial centers for the Navajo reservation as a starting point and make day trips or longer trips onto the Colorado Plateau from there. Most of the main roads through the reservation are paved and open year-round. If you're planning to explore backroads (which may be County or Navajo Routes and are usually dirt roads), make sure you have an up-to-date AAA "Indian Country" map, which shows washes, major rock formations, chapter houses, and other important landmarks on the Navajo reservation.

Road conditions change quickly, especially after rain, making dirt roads impassable. Avoid going offroad unless you have a four-wheel-drive vehicle with good clearance. Stop and ask local Navajos about road conditions. Young people, especially, travel long distances across the Rez each day to jobs miles from their homes and are intimately acquainted with the terrain. Although there are a number of stores and gas stations on the Rez, be as self-sufficient as possible. Keep your gas tank topped up and bring plenty of food and water, and spare tires. Avoid traveling at night. Livestock roam freely on the reservation and can often be found in the road.

Where to start? If you're entering the Navajo Nation in Arizona, you'll find Flagstaff, northern Arizona's biggest town, a good jumping-off point for visits to what's known as the Western Reservation, as well as the adjoining Hopi, Southern Paiute, and Apache reservations. Many Navajo live in Flagstaff, and the Museum of Northern Arizona offers a good orientation to the reservation, as well as the chance to meet Indian artisans at annual juried arts and crafts shows.

US 89 heads north from "Flag," past Sunset Crater and Wupatki National Monuments, and enters the Navajo Nation at Cameron Trading Post National Historic Site. Just before you reach Cameron, you'll pass US 64, the eastern entrance to the Grand Canyon, where you'll find Little Colorado Gorge Navajo Tribal Park. If you stay on Highway 89, heading north, you'll eventually reach Page, headquarters for Glen Canyon National Recreation Area and Lake Powell. You can hire a Navajo guide to visit Antelope Canyon Navajo Tribal Park and Rainbow Bridge National Monument nearby. US 89 continues to Kanab, Utah, a good base for visiting Grand Staircase–Escalante National Monument and Zion National Park.

Alternative route: Turn left onto US 89A at Bitter Springs to visit the North Rim of the Grand Canyon (open May–Oct.). This quiet, paved backroad crosses the Colorado River at Marble Canyon, a good place to stop and buy from Navajo vendors. Nearby is Lee's Ferry, the put-in for river trips through the Grand Canyon. Highway 89 continues over the Kaibab Plateau and down into southern Utah's canyon country, rejoining Highway 89 at Kanab.

Just north of Cameron is the turnoff for US 160, which takes you via Tuba City to Kayenta, a good base for visiting Navajo National Monument, Monument Valley Navajo Tribal Park, and San Juan River communities like Bluff. To visit the Hopi Mesas, turn south on US 264 at Tuba City. This road eventually joins US 191, the main artery linking the North and South Reservations, between US 160 and Interstate 40.

Navajo Highway 12 and US 491, on either side of the Chuska Mountains, along the Arizona–New Mexico border, takes you through the oldest part of the Navajo reservation. If you head northwest from I-40, at Gallup, onto the Defiance Plateau, you'll reach Window Rock, the headquarters of the Navajo Nation. From there, US 264 heads west to Hubbell Trading Post National Historic Site at Ganado, then picks up US 191 north to Canyon de Chelly National Monument at Chinle, and eventually US 160.

On the New Mexico side of the Chuska Mountains, US 491 (the old 666 "Devil's Highway") links Gallup and Shiprock, capital of the Northern Reservation. US 64 continues to the Eastern Reservation, dropping south to I-40 on pretty NM 371 or the faster US 550 to access the Bisti Wilderness and Chaco Canyon. US 550 continues through Cuba and eventually joins I-25, a few miles north of Albuquerque. If you're flying into Albuquerque, US 550 is your best access for the Eastern Reservation.

43

Colorful Lukachukai Dunes and distant buttes.

The Navajo Nation may look like America, but once you enter its boundaries, you are traveling through a sovereign nation, with its own laws and ways of doing things. Remember that you are guest of the Navajo Nation and act accordingly. Take your cue from the people you meet. Although very diverse, many Navajo people are quiet and modest and may not respond to directness and curiosity they consider inappropriate (for example, direct eye contact during conversation and strong handshakes are considered ill-mannered). On the other hand, Navajos have a ripe, earthy sense of humor and love a good joke. Never enter people's houses or land without permission, nor should you photograph Navajo people or ceremonials without prior permission. A small payment is expected if permission is granted.

My best advice for enjoying a trip to the Navajo Nation is to slow down and allow yourself to enter a completely different way of life. It takes time—and willingness—to read other people's cues. But some things are universal. Children, for example. Navajos are inordinately fond of their children, and any show of kindness toward them will be looked on approvingly. Some travelers carry a Polaroid camera and offer instant snapshots to youngsters they meet. Others share pencils, candy, and other treats. It's not about charity; it's about making a human connection. Lastly, the dollars you spend on the reservation are truly needed and appreciated, so plan on buying a piece of jewelry, a rug, a sand painting, even a piece of frybread or a Navajo taco directly from a vendor. It is these personal transactions that will linger in the memory forever—the true meaning of the French word "souvenir."

The Rug Room, Hubbell Trading Post National Historic Site, Arizona.

OF TRADING POSTS AND RUGS

After the Southwest became American territory in 1848, the U.S. Army established forts to defend settlers against Indian incursions. Fort Defiance was built in 1851, shortly after the U.S. government signed a peace treaty with the Navajos. In 1868, as part of the newly established Bureau of Indian Affairs (BIA) Indian Agency, it was the first licensed trading post on the Navajo reservation. It was here that businessmen like Lorenzo Hubbell and Thomas Keam got their start, breaking off to start their own posts in the following decade.

In 1878, Hubbell, the son of an Anglo father and a Mexican mother, opened his first trading post at Ganado, west of Window Rock. He and his two sons would eventually own 30 trading posts. With partner C. N. Cotton, Hubbell reinvigorated the arts and crafts among the Navajos. They hired Mexican silversmiths to teach Navajo men how to work silver and encouraged women to switch from weaving blankets to more saleable rugs and to using naturally dyed wools rather than bright aniline dyes imported from eastern mills. By the early 1900s, catalogs selling various grades of weavings (some by the pound) marketed Hubbell's Ganado rugs as far away as New York City. His biggest buyer was hotelier Fred Harvey who furnished his hotels along the railroad line with Indian art and popularized Indian tourism in the Southwest.

Hubbell Trading Post is now a national historic site. It is little changed from its earliest days. Visitors enter a low, cool, brick building into the

"bullpen," where Bluebird flour, Arbuckle's coffee, tobacco, canned fruit, calico, hardware, and other goods are still prized items among the Navajo. Women continue to bring in rugs they have painstakingly woven—sometimes taking up to a year—to trade for necessities. Seated in a corner of the famed rug room, trader Bill Malone works closely with families, urging women to continue weaving and buying the first efforts of a new generation of weavers, some of them men.

Since the advent of motor cars and good roads, trading posts have declined across the reservation, but individual traders continue their close relationships with local Navajos. The Foutz family run several trading posts in the Shiprock area, including the post at Teec Nos Pos, where the finely woven tapestrylike rugs associated with this area command high prices. Other traders have helped create new markets for Navajo artisans. Trader Bill Beaver at Sacred Mountain Trading Post, north of Flagstaff, has popularized pitch-glazed Navajo ceramics from the Shonto area, including work by Alice Cling, whose fine pottery Beaver likens to the best Hopi pottery. Jim Ostler and Liza Doran of Cow Springs Trading Post and Restaurant in Bluff, Utah, carry a fine collection of Navajo folk art, including whimsical carved sandstone figurines of contemporary Navajos made by the Warren family in Sweetwater. All measure long-term success in terms of loyalty, trust, and acceptance among Navajo families for whom trading posts remain an important part of daily life.

Creative expression comes easily to the Navajo. Inspired by nature and life in remote areas of the reservation, almost every family boasts several weavers, painters, carvers, jewelers, potters, or basketmakers. One of the pleasures of a visit to any part of the Navajo reservation is a chance to meet talented local artisans and buy examples of their work to bring home. There's no shortage of places to purchase Navajo arts and crafts. From ramada vendors in the shadow of Monument Valley and dusty trading posts to museum stores and art galleries, you'll find a bewildering number of items to suit any budget and taste. The first rule of purchasing is to love what you buy, even if it is an investment. The second is to choose a high-quality piece authenticated as Indian-made, preferably with the name of the artist, date, and provenance (keep the tag on). And lastly, remember to have fun.

WEAVING

The Navajo are justly celebrated for their fine woven wool rugs, a skill learned from Pueblo men who wove cotton sashes on upright looms in the kivas. With the arrival of the Spanish in the Southwest, the Navajo began using naturally dyed, long-fibered wool from Spanish *churro* sheep and *bayeta*, a red cloth used in Spanish military uniforms, which weavers unraveled and wove into blankets. During the Classic period, between 1868 and 1880, following the Long Walk, Navajo women used newly available commercial aniline dyes from Germantown, Pennsylvania, to weave bright Eye Dazzler rugs that struck many as garish. Trader Lorenzo Hubbell convinced the weavers to return to traditional patterns using natural dyes, from plants such as rabbitbrush and walnuts,

and to make heavier floor rugs that would appeal more to markets back east.

Particular styles of rug weaving were developed at certain trading posts. They include Ganado and Klagetoh, Teec Nos Pos, Crystal, Chinle, Wide Ruins, Two Grey Hills, and Burntwater, as well as patterns such as storm, twill, tapestry, and mosaic, and pictorial rugs, featuring Yei or Yeibichei dancers and scenes from daily life. Today, Navajos sell at trading posts across the reservation, as well as galleries and museum stores in Southwest cities, such as Albuquerque, Santa Fe, Phoenix, Tucson, Flagstaff, Gallup, Durango, Denver, and Salt Lake City.

Look for soft, smooth, naturally dyed wool rather than bright commercial wools. Rug patterns should be symmetrical, with a tight, even weave. Rugs should lie flat on the floor and not curl up at the corners. Traders say that rug weaving is a dying art, with older weavers frequently unable to pass on their skills to a less interested younger generation. Most encourage young weavers by buying their early efforts (these small rugs are usually available for about $100 and make good starter rugs for your collection, too).

Rugs by well-known weavers cost thousands of dollars. For this kind of investment, learn as much as you can about weaving. For example, Toadlena Trading Post near Newcomb specializes in Two Grey Hills and has a rug museum and demonstrations. For the best deals, attend the monthly Crownpoint Rug Auction, near Gallup, a great way to get to mingle with the Navajo. The biggest prize of all are rare historic rugs, such as Navajo Slave rugs, Eye Dazzlers, early Pictorials, and other patterns. Be sure to work with a reputable dealer if you are interested in collecting these. The best rugs are snapped up quickly.

JEWELRY

"A Navajo wears turquoise so that the Holy People can recognize them," says Elsie Cly, manager of the Navajo Arts and Crafts Enterprise store at Navajo National Monument, one of seven Navajo-owned arts cooperatives on the reservation (the others are in Window Rock, Alamo, Cameron, Chinle, Grants, and Kayenta). Nothing says the Southwest more than turquoise stone, which ranges in color from robin's-egg blue to blue-green. It is shaped by jewelers into disks (*heishi*), nuggets, pendants, and other forms and set into silver to make heavy squash blossom and other styles of necklaces, bracelets, earrings, watch bands, and belt buckles. Natural turquoise often looks slightly blotchy and will change color when it comes into contact with oils or water. Stabilized, enhanced, or fracture-sealed turquoise is manmade; ask before buying.

The Navajo originally learned silversmithing from Mexican artisans in the 1800s. Silver coins from the U.S. government were sewn onto clothing and became a Navajo's personal wealth, snipped

ABOVE: Woman's silver concho belt and red velveteen dress. PHOTO ©STEPHEN TRIMBLE

off and used for purchases or melted down to make silver jewelry. Concho belts, originally made from coins and now made from stamped silver, harken back to that time. The Wheelwright Museum in Santa Fe has a superb collection of Navajo silver, including many decorative spoons.

BASKETS

Round, woven baskets made from sumac are used in Navajo ceremonies, from weddings to Blessingways, and are prized by every family. Baskets are traditionally woven by Navajos and Southern Paiutes on the Shonto Plateau, between Navajo Mountain, Page, and Tuba City. A small tightly woven basket starts at about $100 (you may find some good deals at Crossroads Trading Post on US 98). The best baskets on the reservation can be found at Blue Mountain Trading Post in Blanding and Twin Rocks Trading Post in Bluff, both run by the Simpson family, experts on basketmaking. The Simpsons champion the work of Mexican Hat basketmaker Mary Black, whose award-winning basketry is now nationally known. These two interesting trading posts also specialize in contemporary pictorial and mosaic rugs developed with Navajo artists.

POTTERY

Simple, hand-shaped, pitch-glazed ceramics by potters from the Shonto area are increasingly available on the reservation and in surrounding cities, thanks to the efforts of Bill Beaver of Sacred Mountain Trading Post, north of Flagstaff. Silas and Bertha Claw make unusual pots with effigies of horned toads, figures, and other scenes attached to the out-side. Alice Cling and Faye Tso's pots have an elegant look, sometimes decorated with coils. The pitch glaze and firing techniques give these ceramics a dark, or tawny yellow, shadowed surface that is subtly beautiful.

FOLK ART

In the 1970s, Fruitland resident Mamie Deschillie showed Farmington trader Jack Beasley a whimsical

mud doll that she had made and asked him if he might be interested in selling it. Encouraged by Beasley, Deschillie soon began making decorated mud dolls, quirky animal cutouts with fabric and paint applique, and other home-crafted arts that became a big hit with buyers. Contemporary Navajo folk art by Deschillie, one of the superstars of this popular new trend on the reservation, and a growing number of Central Reservation artists is now some of the most collectible Navajo art in the Southwest.

In Shiprock, Farmington, Bluff, and Blanding, as well at stores in other locations, look for Deschillie's primitive work; beautifully detailed painted cottonwood penknife carvings of contemporary Navajos by Johnson Antonio; figures on horseback by sculptor Delbert Buck; carved and painted sandstone figurines, trucks, horses, and traditional diorama scenes by Homer Warren and family; unique and delicate muslin paintings of ceremonial sand paintings by Bruce and Dennis Hathale; and lifesize board and pelt animals by Ray Growler and family. If you're interested in collecting Navajo art, Navajo folk art is your best bet. The work is delightful, and the prices are still affordable.

PAINTINGS

Navajo artists produce some of the finest drawings, paintings, and sculpture in the Southwest and regularly win awards at the August Santa Fe Indian Market, the biggest and most important juried Indian art show in the country, as well as at smaller shows, such as those held at Museum of Northern Arizona each summer. Harrison Begay attended Santa Fe Indian School with Pueblo painter Pop Chalee and Apache sculptor Allan Houser. His elegant, detailed paintings of Navajo ceremonial dances and other scenes are highly collectible. The humorous paintings and prints of Baje Whitethorne also depict ceremonial dances and life on the reservation and are often used as poster art and in children's books. Look for both men's work at Puchteca Gallery in Flagstaff, Arizona, along with paintings by Shonto Begay, a graduate of Santa Fe's Institute of Indian Arts, whose bright, energetic artwork addresses contemporary problems on the reservation, such as litter and alcoholism. Many people will recognize the highly stylized Navajo women in R. C. Gorman's drawings, paintings, and sculpture, characterized by their resemblance to Asian brushwork paintings. Gorman has his own gallery in downtown Taos, and his work is widely available.

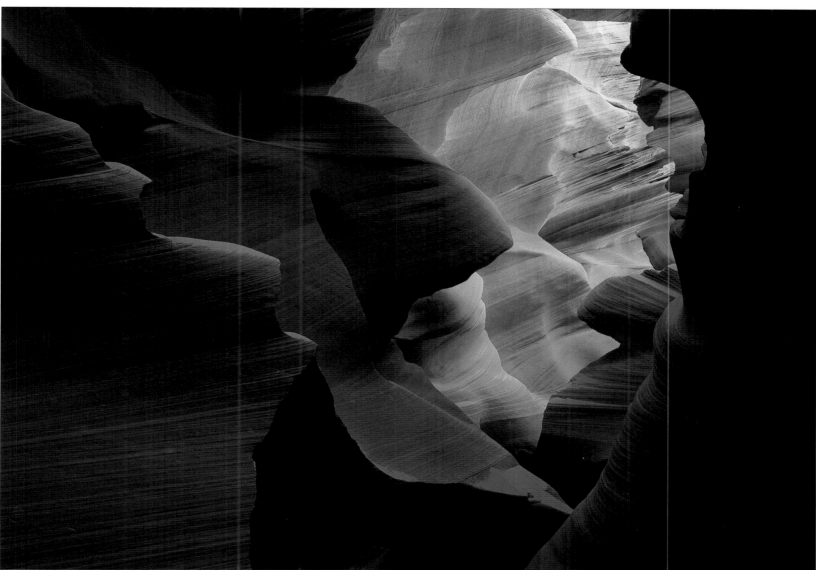

The glowing walls of Lower Antelope Canyon.

PHOTO ©GARY LADD

In 1931, 12-year-old Susie Tsosie was herding sheep between Manson Mesa and Kaibeto, just east of present-day Page, Arizona, when she discovered a half-mile-long, twisting, water-carved crack in the sandstone. Various names have been given to the upper and lower canyons that drain north into Lake Powell. Corkscrew Canyon. Wind Cave. The Crack. But Antelope Canyon is the name that has stuck, a reference to the herds of pronghorn that used to roam freely here.

For photographers, there may be no more compelling place on the Navajo Nation. With walls rising to 120 feet, the canyon is less than 20 feet wide; the sky above disappears at times and sounds are muffled by soft sand underfoot. Light is a reflected memory, illuminating taffy swirls of sandstone. In such places, the creator seems close at hand.

Slot canyons exist in great numbers on the Colorado Plateau, where streams have cut straight down through sandstone. Unlike ordinary erosion, in which rocks of differing compositions and hardness weather into stepped-back cliffs and hoodoos, slot canyons form when the bedrock is uniform from top to bottom. Water entering finds little resistance, and weathering accelerates during times of runoff. Then, with little or no warning, sediment- and debris-laden flashfloods, fueled by unseen storms upcountry, roar through the narrow recesses at the speed of a freight train.

Flashflooding remains a danger in Antelope Canyon. In August 1997, a tour guide and his party of 11 foreign tourists ignored warnings from local Navajos about summer flashflood danger and hiked into Lower Antelope Canyon, the narrower section of the canyon above Lake Powell. All 11 hikers lost their lives when a flashflood swept through the canyon. The only one to survive was the tour guide. A recent flashflood has removed eight feet of sand from the canyon. Be very careful when hiking in these beautiful but deadly places.

The Navajo Parks and Recreation Department now restricts access to Antelope Canyon to travel with a Navajo guide. Three concessionaires in Page offer four-wheel-drive and walking tours of the Upper and Lower Canyons. A 1.5-hour tour of each canyon costs roughly $40 and a five-hour photographers tour costs around $60. You may also drive to the entrance, a mile east of Big Lake Trading Post on US 98, and pay a $6 entry fee at the gate. A concessionaire will then drive you the 3.5 sandy miles to the slot canyon entrance and charge you $15 for a 1.5-hour tour—more for longer tours. This option allows for a more spontaneous trip but may end up costing more than a mainstream tour. It's easy to lose track of time in this cool, cathedral-like canyon, where, as photographer Michael Fatali says, "only our imagination guides us."

OPPOSITE: The water-sculpted walls of Antelope Canyon. PHOTO ©GARY LADD   **PAGE 52/53:** The fantastic erosional forms of Coal Canyon, Arizona. PHOTO ©LARRY ULRICH

Grand Falls of the Little Colorado River after a summer rainstorm.

PHOTO ©TOM BEAN

Arizona's Grand Canyon, centerpiece of the Colorado Plateau, was carved by the Colorado River only within the past 4.7 million–1.7 million years. The ancestral Colorado flowed south into Arizona from Utah, staying east of the Kaibab Upwarp. Another stream flowed west of the Kaibab Upwarp, cut back into the plateau, and "captured" the Colorado, which turned westward to its present position through the newer, steeper route. At this point, sediment-heavy waters began to carve the Grand Canyon, deepening the chasm to its present mile depth.

Spaniards were the first to call the river the Colorado, the "Red River," a reference to the tawny sediments that the river transported all the way to the Gulf of California. Downcutting has slowed now that the river has reached the resistant Vishnu Schist at the bottom of the Grand Canyon and its erosive force has been tamed by Glen Canyon Dam. But weathering has continued to wide the Grand Canyon to its present 10 miles, creating a diz-

zying tributary canyon system surrounded by high ledges, sheer cliffs, dramatic mesas, conical buttes (known as "temples"), and other features.

The Little Colorado River, now occupying the ancestral course of the Colorado, is a major river on the Navajo reservation. It has carved its own beautiful gorge, visible just west of Cameron, off US 64. This gorge—with its sheer, dark walls and gloomy aspect—is quite different from the main canyon. You can view it at an overlook behind Cameron Trading Post Historic Site, where US 89 crosses the river, or at Little Colorado Gorge Navajo Tribal Park, which has picnic ramadas and many Navajo arts and crafts vendors.

For a backroads adventure in early spring or after a major summer rain, consider a drive out to the Grand Falls of the Little Colorado, where floodwaters the color and consistency of frothy milk chocolate cascade dramatically over a 185-foot-high ledge. It's a major undertaking to reach

this little-known scenic spot on the Navajo reservation, but well worth the trek. Take US 89 just north of Flagstaff, turn right onto the Townsend–Winona Road, drive eight miles to Leupp Road, turn left, and then travel another 15 miles to the edge of the Navajo Nation. Turn left (north) onto Navajo Route 70, a decent gravel road that becomes impassable when wet. In another nine miles, you'll reach Grand Falls. Bring everything you need with you; there are no services here.

Within sight of Grand Falls is Roden Crater, which looks like any of a number of cinder cones in the enormous San Francisco Volcanic Field. Appearances are deceptive, though. Since 1977, light artist James Turrell has been transforming this crater into "a large-scale artwork, that relates, through the medium of light, to the universe of the surrounding sky, land, and culture." The scale and ambition of this project is unprecedented. The first public tours of the crater are scheduled for 2005.

Rainbow Bridge and distant, snow-covered Navajo Mountain, Rainbow Bridge National Monument, Arizona.

PHOTO ©GARY LADD

In 1908, surveyor William Douglass pronounced the three rock spans at Natural Bridges National Monument, Utah, the finest and biggest natural bridges in the world. One year later, explorer John Wetherill and two Indians guides—Nasja Begay, a Paiute, and Jim Mike, a Ute— led Douglass and archaeologist Byron Cummings to an even larger and more spectacular natural bridge, just west of the previous three. At a span of 275 feet, 290 feet high, 42 feet thick, and 33 feet wide, it remains the largest known natural bridge on earth.

Rainbow Bridge received its name in honor of a Navajo legend about a young god who was hunting in the canyon and was trapped by floodwaters. The elder gods took pity on him and sent a rainbow to his rescue, on which he climbed to safety. The gods turned the rainbow to stone as proof that they watched over and protected the Dineh.

Geologists say Rainbow Bridge was actually carved by Bridge Creek, which rises on 10,000-foot-high Navajo Mountain and joins the Colorado River to the west. When the Colorado Plateau began rising, the creek cut down in its path and carved a serpentine canyon, helped by seasonal floods and debris that ate through bends in the creek. Known formally as "entrenched meanders," or colloquially as "goosenecks," the riverbends became progressively thinner as the water circled back on itself, finally carving an opening that offered a shortcut for the river and grew into Rainbow Bridge.

All-day boat tours to Rainbow Bridge are offered by concessionaires at Wahweap and Bullfrog Marinas on Lake Powell, but due to the low levels of the lake, you must now hike three miles roundtrip to view the bridge. The only other access is via an unmarked, rugged, 14-mile trail from the Navajo Mountain chapter of the Navajo Nation. Don't attempt this unless you are used to desert hiking, very fit, and able to read a 15-minute quadrangle topo map. For assistance in finding the trail, ask at Navajo Mountain chapter house, located at the end of a long, washboarded road east of US 98. Permits are required. When hiking, carry a gallon of water per person, food, and wear sturdy boots, a broad-brimmed hat, sunglasses, and sunscreen. Rainbow Bridge is sacred to local tribes. Approach it with respect and avoid walking beneath the arch.

Of the many natural bridges in the region, Natural Bridges National Monument, just north of US 95, encompasses the most accessible. Bridge View Drive has overlooks of the three natural bridges in White and Armstrong Canyons as well as Ancestral Pueblo ruins, sacred to the Hopi. Short hiking trails lead from overlooks to the base of Sipapu, Owachomo, and Kachina Bridges, and a nine-mile canyon loop connects all three. The pleasant 13-site campground makes a good base for exploring the area.

WINDOW ROCK
NAVAJO TRIBAL PARK

Veterans Memorial at Window Rock, Arizona.

Window Rock is headquarters for the Navajo Nation. Its name comes from the large, eroded geological window in the Cow Springs Sandstone that overlooks Window Rock Tribal Park. Next door is the Navajo Nation Council Chambers, constructed in the shape of a hogan. Visitors may tour the facility and view council sessions as well as the beautiful mural recounting Dineh history.

Window Rock Tribal Park now includes the Navajo Nation Veterans Memorial. This pretty little downtown park has a circular path outlining the four directions, 16 angled steel pillars with the names of war veterans, and a healing sanctuary with a sandstone fountain that is used for reflection and solitude. Navajos are fiercely proud of their military service record and honor veterans with parades and recognition at many events across the reservation. The tribe's finest hour may have been when Navajo Code Talkers with the U.S. Marine Corps in the Pacific Theater during World War II foiled Japanese codebreakers by transmitting important communications between the allies in Navajo. The code was never broken.

So secret was their work, Code Talkers didn't receive national recognition until 1982, when President Ronald Reagan proclaimed August 14 as National Navajo Code Talkers Day. In 1999, President Bill Clinton visited the reservation and gave a speech that included a few words in Navajo code. For Navajos, the symbolism of that speech lay not so much in recognition of their people's patriotism but in the use of a language that, for many years, the U.S. government had actively worked to stamp out as un-American.

The Navajo Nation Museum, just off US 264—a beautiful, oversized hogan-style cultural center—contains permanent and revolving exhibits interpreting the history of the tribe. Across from the museum, you'll find the Navajo Nation Zoological and Botanical Park, the only tribal zoo in the United States. About 30 species of animal, including mountain lions, coyotes, raptors, and reintroduced Mexican wolves and *churro* sheep, live in naturalistic enclosures. Signs are in English and Navajo and interpret natural history on the Navajo reservation from the Navajo point of view.

Before leaving, be sure to stop next door at the Navajo Parks and Recreation Department for more information on tribal and national parks on the Navajo reservation. Permits for backcountry hiking and camping are required and may be purchased here. Fishing permits are also required and may be purchased at local stores. The helpful staff—several of them veterans of the national park system—will let you know what is going on across the reservation during your visit and can help you plan your trip. The best time to visit Window Rock is during the huge Navajo Nation Fair in September, the world's largest American Indian Fair. Thousands of people pour into town during this four-day event, which includes a popular Pro-Indian rodeo, a powwow, the Miss Navajo Nation pageant, and traditional music, dance, and food.

Traditional hogan at sunset near Aneth, New Mexico.

PHOTO ©BRUCE HUCKO

TONY HILLERMAN AND THE NAVAJO

In 1945, PFC Anthony G. Hillerman, just back from France after receiving the Silver Star on the World War II battlefields, was delivering a truckload of oil field equipment to the Navajo reservation, when he was invited to an Enemy Way, a nine-day cleansing ritual for two Navajo Marines. The ceremony made a huge impression on Hillerman. Twenty-five years later, it would become the centerpiece of *The Blessing Way*, the first of 15 mystery novels set on the Navajo reservation, featuring Navajo Tribal Police officers Joe Leaphorn and Jim Chee.

The Blessing Way established a completely new kind of American detective novel, one where place and culture have equal billing with plot and character. For Hillerman, the modest Anglo son of a poor farmer who grew up during the Depression in the heart of Oklahoma's Indian Territory, the subject matter seemed natural. "I had no trouble at all feeling at home with Navajos," he wrote in his 2001 memoir, *Seldom Disappointed*. "They were the folks I grew up with. . . . [But] even with the knowledge that myth, ceremonials, and taboos vary among the multitude of clans, I was nervous about my role as a white man describing Navajo ways."

After a career as a journalist, Hillerman began writing fiction full-time in 1970. His novels have won acclaim for their unusual plots, meticulous research, and examination of the complexities of modern Indian life. In Hillerman Country, sacred peaks, remote canyons, scattered sheep camps, creaky trading posts, secret ceremonies, and feared Navajo witches are as much a reality as modern reservation towns like Shiprock and Window Rock, tent revivals, jobs in coal mines and other industries, Burger King and Wal-Mart, and youngsters more familiar with sports, rock music, and the Internet than the Navajo language and traditional lifeways of their elders.

Over the years, Hillerman has tackled topics as diverse as the theft and return of archaeological remains, Indian casino holdups, pillaging of natural resources, the clash of federal and tribal authority, Navajo relations with Ute, Apache, Hopi, Zuni, and Tohono O'odham neighbors, and the influence of Anglo ranchers, miners, missionaries, doctors, and teachers. Center stage is the relationship between ex-anthropologist Leaphorn, a widower easing into retirement after a distinguished career with the Navajo Tribal Police, and Jim Chee, an intense young cop equally torn between police work, training as a medicine man, and romances with women as diverse as an Anglo teacher, a Navajo lawyer, and a fellow cop.

Hillerman has won numerous awards over the years, but he is most proud of receiving the Navajo Nation's prestigious "Special Friend of the Dineh" plaque, awarded as "an expression of appreciation and friendship for authentically portraying the strength and dignity of traditional Navajo culture." For Hillerman, a down-to-earth family man whose life, as he says, has been blessed repeatedly, nothing could be more meaningful.

Badlands of Bisti Wilderness.　PHOTO ©TOM TILL

Dinosaur tracks near Cameron, AZ.　PHOTO ©TOM BEAN

Blue Mesa, Petrified Forest.　PHOTO ©GARY LADD

BISTI/DE-NA-ZIN WILDERNESS

The Bisti/De-Na-Zin Wilderness encompasses 45,000 acres of remote badlands, 20 miles south of Farmington, off NM 371. The wilderness was set aside in 1996 to protect its important record of changes in plant and animal life at the end of the Age of Dinosaurs, 65 million years ago. The Fruitland Formation and Kirtland Shale were laid down in coastal swamps and contain sandstone, shale, mudstone, coal, and silt that have been eroded into spires, toadstool-shaped hoodoos, and crumbly hills turned bright red from subterranean coal fires millennia ago. Numerous fossils have been found here, including duck-billed dinosaurs and petrified wood. Administered by the BLM, the Bisti (Bis-tie) and De-Na-Zin (named for petroglyphs of cranes found south of the site) have no services and can only be entered on foot. Bring food, water, sun protection, and let someone know where you are. Several dirt county roads (impassable after rain) lead from the wilderness to Chaco Culture National Historical Park.

BOWL CANYON–ASAAYI LAKE RECREATION AREA

Navajo Parks and Recreation in Window Rock administers eight tribal parks, including this recreation area in the lovely Chuska Mountains, where you can hike, camp, picnic, fish, canoe, and watch wildlife next to a pristine mountain lake. Two hiking trails wind through the sandstone monoliths of Bowl Canyon. Thirty-six-acre Asaayi Lake is one of several alpine lakes on the Navajo reservation stocked with trout; the others are Todacheene Lake, Whiskey Lake, Berland Lake, Long Lake, and Aspen Lake. Adjoining Camp Asaayi is used by groups and has open-air cabins, a kitchen, dining hall, and sports facilties. To reach the lake, head north on Navajo 12 and turn right at NM 134 onto Narbona Pass. Asaayi Lake is just past Crystal on the right, at the end of a seven-mile dirt road. **Note:** Be sure to stop in Window Rock to pick up a permit to use this park.

DINOSAUR TRACKS

Dinosaur trackways are abundant in the Four Corners region of the Navajo reservation, where erosion has uncovered footprints from a variety of dinosaurs that once ruled the swamps of equatorial western America. One of the best trackways lies just north of US 160, just beyond the turnoff from US 89 for Tuba City. Handmade signs lead to the spot where, 200 million years ago, a three-toed dilophosaurus, or "running dinosaur," ran on its hind legs through interdunal swamps, leaving behind clear tracks in the red Kayenta Formation. Weighing 1,000 pounds and standing 8 to 10 feet tall, dilophosaurus used short forearms and clawed fingers for grasping and tearing apart its prey. Claw marks can be seen in the tracks. For a few dollars, a young Navajo guide will show you the tracks.

FOUR CORNERS MONUMENT NAVAJO TRIBAL PARK

This unique park, six miles north of Teec Nos Pos and US 160, is the only place in the United States where four states (New Mexico, Colorado, Utah, and Arizona) come together. It is also the only place where two Indian reservations adjoin each other. The monument was surveyed and established by U.S. government surveyors and astronomers, starting with Ehud Darling in Colorado in 1868, Chandler Robbins in New Mexico and Rollin Reeves in Utah in 1878, and Howard Carpenter in Arizona in 1901. A cadastral marker made of granite, bronze disc, and colored concrete has now replaced the original, plain concrete 1912 marker. The Navajo Nation charges a small entrance fee. There is a modest visitor center but no water. Vendors from local Navajo and Ute Mountain Ute families sell fry bread and arts and crafts. Open May–Aug., 7 a.m.–8 p.m., 8 a.m.–5 p.m. in winter.

PETRIFIED FOREST NATIONAL PARK

Petrified Forest National Park preserves 147 square miles of the Painted Desert, a breathtaking high-desert

Homolovi State Park. PHOTO ©GEORGE H. H. HUEY

Kin Yahzi Ruin, Navajo Pueblito. PHOTO ©BOB YOUNG

Hogan and Ship Rock. PHOTO ©STEPHEN TRIMBLE

landscape of buttes, mesas, and banded pink, brown, gray, and purple Chinle Formation badlands spanning Interstate 40, on the southern boundary of the Navajo Nation, 20 miles east of Holbrook, Arizona. The park was set aside in 1906 to protect one of the world's largest deposits of petrified wood, which formed 225 million years ago, when North America was about where West Africa is today. Dinosaurs, such as the ferocious-looking phytosaur, populated tropical swamps, along with enormous cycad ferns and 200-feet-high conifers. When these conifers toppled into tropical swamps, they were buried by silt and ash from volcanoes to the south. Silicates gradually mixed with groundwater and replaced woody cells with jasper, amethyst, and smokey quartz, creating fossilized wood. A 27-mile scenic drive has pullouts and interpretive displays on petrified wood, the 100-room Anasazi ruin of Puerco Pueblo, and a spectacular petroglyph display. Rainbow Forest Museum, at the south entrance, and historic Painted Desert Inn Museum (open summer only), at Kachina Point, have exhibits. There are no developed campgrounds or trails, but you may hike and camp in the wilderness areas of the park with a backcountry permit. Avoid summer heat; there is no shade here.

HOMOLOVI RUINS STATE PARK

Certain clans of the Hopi tribe, whose homes lie on the Hopi Mesas 60 miles to the north, cite Homolovi Ruins State Park, near Winslow, as an ancestral Pueblo home. The park preserves several 14th-century pueblos atop high mounds overlooking the Painted Desert and a large number of petroglyph panels etched on volcanic rocks. Homolovi I and II are the only sites accessible to visitors. The park has hiking trails, a campground, picnic areas, a scenic drive, and an attractive air-conditioned visitor center. It is open daily 8 a.m.–5 p.m. and an entrance fee is charged.

PUEBLITOS OF THE DINETAH

The remains of small Navajo stone villages, known as pueblitos, dot rugged and remote Gobernador and Largo Canyons in the former Navajo homeland of the Dinetah in northeastern New Mexico. Built in the 17th and 18th centuries, as a defense against Ute and Spanish slave raiding, these fortified walled buildings are unique historic structures, combining Pueblo and Spanish architecture with rare, old-style Navajo forked hogans. Archaeologists have found 100 pueblitos to date, along with extraordinary panels of Navajo petroglyphs featuring deities, corn, and other sacred subjects. Two of the largest ruins—Three Corn Ruin and Truby's Tower—are now on the list of the most-endangered sites in New Mexico. Guided tours can be arranged through San Juan County Archaeological Research Center at Salmon Ruin in Bloomfield; tel. 505-632-2013. Salmon Ruin is a county park preserving a 217-room Chaco Anasazi great house along the San Juan River built in A.D. 1088. The attractive kiva-shaped visitor center has a museum with exhibits and a computer program that allows visitors to do a virtual tour of 16 Chacoan satellite communities, or outliers. Open daily 9 a.m.–5 p.m.

SHIP ROCK

The 1,000-foot-high volcanic neck, or diatreme, known as Ship Rock is located just south of the San Juan River in the Four Corners. To the Navajo, it is *Tse Bitai*, "the Rock with Wings," the man-eating eagle monster turned to stone by Monster Slayer in the Navajo creation story. Geologists say it is the remnant of a volcanic eruption that never surfaced but has been uncovered by erosion. The rock is sacred, and no one may climb it. The nearby town of the same name, Shiprock, is the capital of the Northern Reservation and home of Shiprock High School's women's basketball team, the Lady Chieftains, which won the state basketball championships in the 1980s with the help of their African-American coach. The Northern Navajo Nation Fair is held in Shiprock every October.

Sheep being herded at Sand Springs Dunes, Monument Valley.

THE NAVAJO TODAY

By the 1930s, the Dineh's success in restocking the range and rebuilding their population had begun to work against them. Their reservation was too small to support large numbers of stock, and rangelands became overgrazed during drought conditions. Government-mandated stock reductions backfired when officials bypassed Navajo women, who own the stock, and dealt with the men. The resulting slaughter still evokes painful memories among elderly Navajos.

Traditional lifeways in general are in decline. For a century, education in government-run boarding schools emphasized assimilation. Indian children were separated from their families, dressed in Anglo clothes, prepared for work as maids and laborers, and punished for speaking their native tongue. Things looked so dire in the 1930s that Mary Cabot Wheelwright and trader Franc Newcomb worked with Navajo medicine man Hosteen Klah to found the Museum of Navajo Ceremonial Art (now the Wheelwright Museum) in Santa Fe to record Navajo ritual knowledge before it died out.

Navajo culture has been dealt an additional blow by the Navajo-Hopi Land Dispute, a century-long boundary disagreement between the Hopi and Navajo tribes. Following a court decision in 1974, thousands of traditional Western Navajos have been forced to relocate from hogans to houses in Flagstaff and other cities, with predictably tragic consequences. Residents at Big Mountain continue to fight relocation, but the government and the Hopi tribe show no signs of backing down.

Navajo leader Manuelito's vision for a better-educated tribe making their own decisions has largely come to pass, however. Children now attend day schools on or near the reservation, and in 1968, Navajo Community College,

the first Indian-run college in the nation, was founded at Tsaile. NCC teaches both mainstream subjects and Navajo culture, including the Navajo language, ceremonials, art, and animal husbandry. Navajos now fill numerous administrative jobs on the reservation, although unemployment remains high. The tribe has rejected casino gambling in favor of heritage tourism. Efforts to promote small businesses, tribal and national parks, and the new Antelope Point Marina on Lake Powell seem to be paying off.

Far more difficult to address, however, are the environmental problems caused by industrial facilities on the reservation. Uranium mining in the Chuska Mountains, Monument Valley, Tuba City, and Shiprock was widespread throughout the Cold War. On July 16, 1979, the biggest explosion of radioactive waste in U.S. history occurred at Church Rock, near Grants, spewing 1,100 tons of polluted mud and water into the Rio Puerco. Cancer among former workers and families living nearby has been ignored for years, although recently, grassroots activists have succeeded in getting government officials to acknowledge the problem and begin financial reparations for victims.

Efforts to improve the environment for Navajo and Hopi families living on Black Mesa continue to face an uphill battle. Since 1970, Peabody Coal Company has strip-mined coal on Black Mesa, draining millions of gallons of pristine groundwater to create slurry that is transported via pipeline to Mohave Generating Station in Laughlin, Nevada, to power California homes. Peabody's lease with the tribes is up for renewal in 2005. In June 2004, activists succeeded in getting California Edison Company to rewrite its agreement with Peabody to require new sources of groundwater for slurried coal or shut down Mohave Generating Station. To date, no agreement on alternative sources of water has been reached.

MAY

ANNUAL SHIPROCK MARATHON, RELAY, AND HALF MARATHON WALK
Shiprock, New Mexico
(505) 368-3523; e-mail:cbates@shiprock.ncc.cc.nm.us
www.shiprock.ncc.cc.nm.us

NATIVE AMERICAN ARTS AUCTION
Hubbell Trading Post
Ganado, Arizona
400 items for sale—historic and contemporary Native American Arts.
Viewing 9am-11am. Auction 12-5pm.
(928) 755-3475
e-mail:
e_chamberlin@nps.gov
www.nps.gov/hutr

JUNE

ANNUAL MUSIC FESTIVAL
Navajo Nation Museum
Window Rock, AZ
Includes art and craft vendors, book signing, and other exciting activities.
(928) 810-8540

JULY

FOURTH OF JULY CELEBRATION
Window Rock, AZ
Professional Rodeo Cowboys Association (PRCA) Rodeo, carnival, traditional Navajo song and dance, concerts, arts and crafts sales and fireworks.
Contact: Navajo Nation Fair: (928) 871-6647
www.navajonationparks.org

EASTERN NAVAJO FAIR
Crownpoint, New Mexico.
Contact Crownpoint Chapter. (505) 786-2130
www.navajonationparks.org

AUGUST

ANNUAL NAVAJO ARTS AND CRAFTS SHOW
Museum of Northern Arizona,
Flagstaff, Arizona
(928) 774-5213

INTER-TRIBAL INDIAN CEREMONIAL
Red Rock State Park
Near Gallup, New Mexico.
A huge powwow with arts and crafts shows, parades, rodeo, and more.
(505) 722-3829

SANTE FE INDIAN MARKET
The largest and oldest open-air juried Indian Market in the country. On Santa Fe Plaza, Santa Fe, New Mexico.
(505) 983-5220

ANNUAL PIONEER CELEBRATION
Navajo Mountain, Utah
Foot races, traditional Navajo games and food, talent show, entertainment for children, adults and senior citizens, 5k/10k run Saturday morning; main event 8am to 4pm. Volleyball tournament: Saturday evening and Sunday.
Contact:
Navajo Mountain Chapter: (928) 672-2857

ANNUAL INTERNATIONAL SPIRITUAL GATHERING
Rocksprings, New Mexico.
Spiritual prayers, Pow-wows, traditional Navajo song and dance, arts and crafts sale, rodeo, and more family fun.

Free admission.
1.5 mile north of Rocksprings Chapter.
(505) 722-2177

CENTRAL NAVAJO FAIR
Chinle, Arizona
Contact: Chinle Chapter: (928) 674-2052

NATIVE AMERICAN ARTS AUCTION
Hubbell Trading Post
Ganado, Arizona
400 items for sale—historic and contemporary Native American Arts. Viewing 9am-11am. Auction 12-5pm.
(928) 755-3475; e-mail: e_chamberlin@nps.gov
www.nps.gov/hutr

ANNUAL RAMAH NAVAJO FAIR & RODEO
Pine Hill, New Mexico.
Carnival,Team Roping; NNRCA Rodeo; IJRA Rodeo & Pow Wow; Open Show Rodeo; Queen Pageants, 5K Run/Walk, Parade, Barbeque and C&W dance.
(505) 775-3256 or 505-775-3226

SEPTEMBER

ANNUAL NAVAJO NATION FAIR
"The World's Largest American Indian Fair"
Red Rock State Park
Near Gallup, New Mexico.
Multi-Sanctioned Indian Rodeo, carnival, traditional Navajo song & dance, inter-tribal pow-wow, traditional Navajo food, concerts, parade, children's day, Miss Navajo Nation Pageant, agricultural & commercial exhibits, and a free barbecue.
Contact: Navajo Fair Office.
(928) 871-6478/6702
www.navajonationparks.org

UTAH NAVAJO FAIR
Bluff, Utah
Contact Red Mesa Chapter.
(928) 656-3655

OCTOBER

NORTHERN NAVAJO FAIR
Shiprock, New Mexico
(Always begins on the first Thursday in October)
Contact:
Shiprock Chapter.
(505)368-1089

ALAMO INDIAN DAY
Alamo, New Mexico.
Parade, Indian Market, Pow-wow, traditional Navajo song and dance, Navajo food, Miss Alamo Indian Pageant and arts and crafts.
Contact:
Wanda Apachito, Alamo Chapter.
(505) 854-2686/2688

WESTERN NAVAJO FAIR
Tuba City, Arizona
Contact: Tuba City Chapter. (928) 283-3284

NOVEMBER

ANNUAL NAVAJO NATION MUSEUM KESHMISH FESTIVAL
Window Rock, AZ.
This event highlights emerging and established artists for fine design and quality workmanship in jewelry, weaving, clothing, pottery, paintings, carvings, sculpture, and other art forms. The festival includes cultural events and entertainment.
Contact Navajo Nation Museum.
(928) 871-6029.

ABOVE: Young dancer at Navajo Fair, Window Rock, Arizona. PHOTO ©TOM BEAN

RESOURCES AND INFORMATION

EMERGENCY AND MEDICAL
24-HOUR EMERGENCY MEDICAL SERVICE
Dial 911

ROAD CONDITIONS
Arizona   (888) 411-7623
New Mexico   (800) 432-4269
Utah   (800) 492-2400

MORE INFORMATION
NAVAJO NATION
P.O. Box 308
Window Rock, AZ 86515
(928) 871-6352
www.navajo.org
NAVAJOLAND
TOURISM
P.O. Box 663
Window Rock, AZ 86515
(928) 871-6436/7371
www.discovernavajo.com
NAVAJO PARKS AND
RECREATION
P.O. Box 9000
Window Rock, AZ 86515
(928) 871-6647
www.navajonationparks.org
NAVAJO FISH AND
WILDLIFE DEPARTMENT
P.O. Box 1480
Window Rock, AZ 86515
(928) 871-6451/6452
NAVAJO OFFICE OF
BROADCAST SERVICES
P.O. Box 2310
Window Rock, AZ 86515
Note: Permits for
commercial photography
and filming must be
secured in advance.
KAYENTA
VISITOR CENTER
P.O. Box 545,
Kayenta, AZ 86033
(928) 697-3572
MONUMENT VALLEY
NAVAJO TRIBAL PARK
P.O. Box 360289
Monument Valley, UT 84536
(435) 727-5870
NAVAJO PARK TRADING POST
P.O. Box 360457
Monument Valley, UT 84536
(435) 727-3468
E-mail: navajoparktradingpost@frontier.net

TOUR GUIDES
Tour guides can be hired at most visitor attractions on the
Navajo Nation. The following are licensed with the tribe.
GOULDING'S MONUMENT VALLEY TOURS
P.O. Box 3600001
Monument Valley, UT 84536
(800) 874-0902 or 435-727-3231
SIMPSON'S TRAILHANDLER TOURS
P.O. Box 360377
Monument Valley, UT 84536
(435) 727-3362
www.trailhandlertours.com

CRAWLEYS MONUMENT VALLEY TOURS
P.O. Box 187
Kayenta, AZ 86033
(928) 697-3734
DE CHELLY TOURS
P.O. Box 2539
Chinle, AZ 86503
(928) 674-3772
NAVA–HOPI TOURS
P.O. Box 339
Flagstaff, AZ 86002
(928) 774-5003

LARGO NAVAJOLAND TOURS
P.O. Box 3244
Gallup, NM 87305
(888) 726-9084
www.navajolandtours.com
FAR HORIZONS ARCHAEOLOGICAL
AND CULTURAL TRIPS
P.O. Box 91900
Albuquerque, NM 87199
(800) 552-4575
www.farhorizon.com

LODGING
GOULDING'S LODGE
P.O. Box 1
Monument Valley, UT 84536
(435) 727-3231
NAVAJO NATION INN
Box 2340
Window Rock, AZ 86515
(800) 237-7506

THUNDERBIRD LODGE
P.O. Box 548
Chinle, AZ 86503
(800) 679-2473
KAYENTA HOLIDAY INN
P.O. Box 307
Kayenta, AZ 86033
(928) 697-3221
TUBA MOTEL
P.O. Box 247
Tuba City, AZ 86045
(928) 283-4545

COYOTE PASS
HOSPITALITY
(Hogan stays and tours near
Canyon de Chelly)
Rt. 12, P.O. Box 91-B
Tsaile, AZ 86556
(520) 724-3383
CAMERON MOTEL
P.O. Box 339
Cameron, AZ 86020
(800) 338-7385
EL RANCHO HOTEL
1000 East 66 Avenue
Gallup, NM 87301
(800) 543-6351

CAMPGROUNDS
Available at national, state,
and tribal parks, including:
MITTENS VIEW
CAMPGROUND
Monument Valley, Utah
(435) 727-3287
GOULDINGS
CAMPGROUND
Monument Valley, Utah
(435) 727-3231
RED ROCK STATE PARK
NM 56, off I-40, near
Gallup, New Mexico
(505) 722-3829

OTHER REGIONAL SITES
CANYON DE CHELLY
NATIONAL MONUMENT
P.O. Box 588
Chinle, AZ 86503
(928) 674-5500
www.nps.gov/cach
CHACO CULTURE
NATIONAL HISTORICAL PARK
P.O. Box 220
Nageezi, NM 87037
(505) 786-7014
GLEN CANYON
NATIONAL RECREATION AREA
P.O. Box 1507
Page, AZ 86040
(928) 645-2471
HOMOLOVI RUINS STATE PARK
HCR 63, Box 5
Winslow, AZ 86047
(928) 289-4106

ABOVE: Late afternoon in Mystery Valley, buttes of Monument Valley are visible in background. PHOTO ©CHUCK LAWSEN

**HUBBELL TRADING POST
NATIONAL HISTORIC SITE**
P.O. Box 150
Ganado, AZ 86505
(928) 755-3405
www.nps.gov/hutr

**NAVAJO NATIONAL
MONUMENT**
HC-71, Box 3
Tonalea, AZ 86044
(928) 672-2700
www.nps.gov/nava

**PETRIFIED FOREST
NATIONAL PARK**
P.O. Box 2217
Petrified Forest
National Park, AZ 86028
(928) 524-6228
www.nps.gov/pefo

**RAINBOW BRIDGE
NATIONAL MONUMENT**
P.O. Box 1507
Page, AZ 86040
(928) 645-2471

RUG AUCTIONS
**CROWNPOINT RUG
AUCTION**
Crownpoint Elementary
Crownpoint, NM.
(505) 786-7386.
www.crownpointrugauction.com
Usually held on the second
Friday of each month.
Viewing 4:30–6:30 pm.
Auction at 7:00 p.m.
prompt. Arrive early.

**HUBBELL TRADING
POST NATIONAL
HISTORICAL PARK**
Ganado, Arizona
(928) 755-3475.
www.nps.gov/hutr
American Indian arts
auction held twice a year.
Four hundred historic and
contemporary items for
sale. Viewing 9am–11am. Auction 12–5pm.

MUSEUMS
NAVAJO NATION MUSEUM
NR 264, Loop Road
Window Rock, AZ
(928) 871-6673 (recording)

**NED A. HATATHLI
CULTURAL CENTER MUSEUM AND GALLERY**
Navajo Community College
Route 12, 1 Circle, Tsaile, AZ
(928) 724-6600 x 6653

MUSEUM OF NORTHERN ARIZONA
3101 North Fort Valley Road
Flagstaff, AZ 86001
928-774-5213

NOTAH DINEH
345 W. Main
Cortez, CO 81321
(970) 565-9607

**TOADLENA TRADING POST
AND WEAVING MUSEUM**
P.O. Box 8014
Newcomb, NM 87455
(888) 420-0005

**WHEELWRIGHT MUSEUM
OF THE AMERICAN INDIAN**
704 Camino Lejo
Santa Fe, NM 87501
(800) 607-4636
www.wheelwright.org

SUGGESTED READING
Bahti, Mark. *A Consumer's Guide to Southwestern Indian Arts and Crafts.* Tucson, AZ: Bahti Indian Arts. 1975.
Bulow, Ernie. *Navajo Taboos.* Gallup, NM: Buffalo Medicine Books. 1991.
Clark, Jackson H. Foreword by Terry Tempest Williams. *The Owl in Monument Canyon and Other Stories from Indian Country.* Salt Lake City, UT: University of Utah Press. 1993.
Gilpin, Laura. *The Enduring Navajo.* Austin, TX: University of Texas. 1968.
Grimes, Joel. *Navajo: Portrait of a Nation.* Englewood, CO: Westcliffe Publishers. 1992.
Hooker, Kathy Eckles. *Time Among the Navajo: Traditional Lifeways on the Reservation.* Santa Fe, NM : Museum of New Mexico Press. 1991.
Houk, Rose. *Canyon de Chelly.* Tucson, AZ: Southwest Parks and Monuments Association.
Hillerman, Tony. *Seldom Disappointed: A Memoir.* San Francisco, CA: HarperCollins. 2001.
Hillerman, Tony. *A Thief of Time.* New York, NY: Harper and Row. 1988.

Jacka Jerry and Lois. *Beyond Tradition: Contemporary Indian Art and its Evolution.* Flagstaff, AZ: Northland Publishing. 1988.
Kawano, Kenji. *Warriors: Navajo Code Talkers.* New York, NY: Abradale Press.1990.
Kent, Kate Peck. *Navajo Weaving: Three Centuries of Change.* Santa Fe, NM: School of American Research Press. 1985.
Kosik, Fran. *Native Roads: The Complete Motoring Guide to the Navajo and Hopi Nations.* Flagstaff, AZ: Creative Solutions Publishing. 1996.
Leach, Nicky. *The Guide to National Parks of the Southwest.* Tucson, AZ: Southwest Parks and Monuments Association. 1992.
Locke, Raymond Friday. *The Book of the Navajo,* 5th Edition. Los Angeles, CA: Mankind Publishing. 1992.
McNitt, Frank. *The Indian Traders.* Norman, OK: University of Oklahoma Press. 1962.
Newcomb, Franc Johnson. *Navajo Neighbors.* Norman, OK: University of Oklahoma Press. 1966.
Newcomb, Franc Johnson. *Navajo Folk Tales.* Albuquerque, NM: University of New Mexico Press, 1990.
Newcomb, Franc Johnson. *Hosteen Klah: Navajo Medicine Man and Sand Painter.* Norman, OK: University of Oklahoma Press. 1964.
Rosenak, Chuck and Jan. *The People Speak: Navajo Folk Art.* Flagstaff, AZ: Northland Publishing. 1994
Stories from the Long Walk. Various authors. Tsaile, AZ: Navajo Community College.
Wetherill, Marietta. *Reflections on Life with the Navajo in Chaco Canyon.* Edited and compiled by Kathryn Gabriel. Introductory essay by Elizabeth Jameson. Boulder, CO: Johnson Books. 1992.
Williams, Terry Tempest. *Pieces of White Shell: A Journey to Navajoland.* Illustrations by Clifford Brycelea. New York, NY: Scribner. 1984.

ABOVE: Dramatic light on Leaning Butte, near Many Farms, Arizona. PHOTO ©STEVE MOHLENKAMP

ACKNOWLEDGMENTS

A-hay-hay (thank you) to the many Dineh who continue to share information about their culture with me. A particular thank you to Martin Begay at Navajo Parks and Recreation, which works hard to preserve and interpret the many stunning Navajo tribal lands of *Dineh Bikeyah,* for his review of this text; Wilson Hunter, Chief of Interpretation at Canyon de Chelly National Monument, who was helpful with information and resources; and James Charles, former superintendent of Navajo National Monument, who gave me an evening tour of Betatakin Pueblo on my birthday that was truly the icing on the cake. Lastly, every writer should be lucky enough to have as supportive a publisher and friend as Sierra Press's Jeff Nicholas in their corner, especially when things get tough. Jeff saw the potential in this book and enthusiastically let me "have at it" over a most enjoyable year. I've said it before, and I'll say it again: You're the best!   —N.L.

PRODUCTION CREDITS

Publisher: Jeff D. Nicholas
Author: Nicky Leach
Editor: Cindy Bohn
Illustrations: Darlece Cleveland
Printing Coordination: Sung In Printing America

ISBN 1-58071-059-X (Paper)
          1-58071-060-3 (Cloth)
©2005 Sierra Press.

SIERRA PRESS

4988 Gold Leaf Drive, Mariposa, CA 95338
(209) 966-5071, 966-5073 (Fax)
e-mail: siepress@sti.net

BELOW
Yucca near fog-shrouded Three Sisters, winter in Monument Valley. PHOTO ©JACK DYKINGA
OPPOSITE
Monument Valley as seen from atop Hunt's Mesa.
PHOTO ©KERRICK JAMES